Trends and issues in technical and
vocational education 2

Titles in this series:

1. *Developments in Technical and Vocational Education: A Comparative Study* (also published in French and Spanish)
2. *The Transition from Technical and Vocational Schools to Work*
3. *The Integration of General and Technical and Vocational Education*

The transition from technical and vocational schools to work

Problems, current efforts and innovative
approaches and measures
for improving the transition

A summary report of
an international symposium
and seventeen country reports

Unesco

Published in 1983 by the United Nations
Educational, Scientific and Cultural Organization
7 place de Fontenoy, 75700 Paris
Composition by Solent Typesetting Ltd, Otterbourne, United Kingdom
Printed by Imprimerie de la Manutention, Mayenne

ISBN 92-3-102030-7

© Unesco 1983
Printed in France

Preface

The transition from technical and vocational schools to the world of work has long been considered a critical problem area in Member States. Many attempts have been made to smooth this transition and the approaches taken vary considerably from country to country.

One Unesco activity in this field was the international symposium convened by the Organization in Berlin (capital of the German Democratic Republic) from 14 to 18 April 1980.

Seventeen national specialists, nominated by Member States, participated presenting reports on the situation in their countries, while the Unesco Secretariat prepared a working document to serve as a discussion guide.

The present publication, compiled by Dr Daniel B. Dunham, Deputy United States Commissioner for Education, is a summary report based on these materials. It should be of interest to policy-makers and administrators responsible for planning economic and social policy, for labour and employment, and for the various occupational sectors (industry, agriculture, commerce); bodies responsible for out-of-school education and training; representatives of those responsible – both in public education and in state-recognized private education – for implementing policy, including teachers, examining bodies and administrators; and parent, former-pupil, student and youth organizations.

Unesco wishes to express its gratitude to all those who prepared country reports, and to thank in particular Dr Dunham.

The views expressed in this book are those of the individuals concerned and not necessarily those of Unesco. The designations employed and the presentation of the material do not imply the expression of any opinion whatsoever on the part of the Unesco Secretariat concerning the legal status of any country, territory, city or area or of its authorities, or concerning the delimitation of its frontiers or boundaries.

Contents

1. Introduction   9
2. Nature and scope of the problem   13
3. Current efforts and innovative approaches   21
4. Measures for improving the transition   58
5. Conclusions   70

Appendixes
1. Revised Recommendation concerning Technical and Vocational Education   75
2. Guidelines for preparing country reports to be presented to the symposium on problems of transition from technical and vocational schools to work   94
3. International Symposium on Problems of Transition from Technical and Vocational Schools to Work (Berlin, German Democratic Republic), 14 – 18 April 1980. Summary of discussions   96
4. List of authors of country reports   100

1 Introduction

This final report of the Unesco Symposium on Problems of Transition from Technical and Vocational Schools to Work relates the discussions of the symposium itself and summarizes the essential information from the country reports provided by participating Member States.

The contents of this report are drawn primarily from the country reports, with supplementary information from the symposium's initial summary (Appendix 3) and certain working papers provided to participants.

The Unesco Revised Recommendation on Technical and Vocational Education (Appendix 1) provided important guidance to the formation of the report in terms of basic principles and elements which are intended to assist Member States as they seek to resolve problems surrounding the topic of technical and vocational education.

Seventeen countries participated in the symposium, representing a cross section of developing nations, industrialized nations and those in the centre of the scale. In size, they ranged from the island nation of Barbados to the Union of Soviet Socialist Republics. Political, social and government make-up was highly diverse, as can be seen from the following listing of participating countries: Algeria, Australia, Barbados, Democratic People's Republic of Korea, Ethiopia, France, German Democratic Republic, Federal Republic of Germany, India, Iraq, Nigeria, Senegal, Sudan, Sweden, Thailand, Union of Soviet Socialist Republics, United States of America.

The country reports were designed to inform participants of developments in technical and vocational education in the respective country, with a view to facilitating the exchange of information and discussion at the symposium on the subject of transition from technical and vocational schools to work. Guidelines provided by the Unesco Secretariat for the development of the country report requested the following of the country reports:
1. Overall structure of the country's education system and the place of technical and vocational education, including teacher training, within that country. Papers were also to reveal overall policy-making and planning for technical and vocational education; research and curriculum development and methods for the collection and dissemination of information; co-ordination mechanisms between in- and out-of-school programmes, including

linkages with manpower planning and employment in general; and the structure of the vocational and educational guidance programme, whether established within or outside the system of education.
2. Organizational measures taken by the reporting country to facilitate the transition from technical and vocational schools to work, including manpower surveys; co-ordinating mechanisms with industry; work-study arrangements; physical placement of schools in relation to employment demand; and follow-up systems after graduation or the completion of schooling.
3. Methods and their content as utilized in relation to vocational guidance, as well as steps taken to increase the relevancy of curriculum and teaching to employment; and discussion of research undertaken to increase the employment opportunities for graduates of vocational and technical schools.
4. Teaching staff, including identification of whether separate guidance teachers are employed and if so, how they are trained; use of teachers from business and industry on a part-time basis; and the extent of the involvement of teachers in co-ordination and co-operation between schools and employers during the transition period.
5. Conclusions regarding the major achievement of the country on the problems of transition from technical and vocational schools to work, with indication of drawbacks and difficulties encountered and the actions planned to offset them.

In general, the country reports followed the suggested format. Thus, it was possible to review all available reports in a reasonably consistent manner for the purposes of preparing this report. Where there are significant variances from the suggested format, no attempt is made to speculate as to what the report might have stated. Each report is respected for its individual integrity and is accepted as factual. Where data or information are insufficient to secure findings from a given country report, none are provided in this report. For more specific study, the country reports are available through Unesco, Paris, or from the ERIC Clearinghouse for Vocational, Career and Adult Education at the Ohio State University, Columbus, Ohio, United States of America. The latter are available in microfiche form.

The purpose of this report is to synthesize and summarize essential information from the country reports, the initial summary of symposium discussions, and other documents related to the symposium under three major subheadings, each representing a chapter of the report, as follows: (a) nature and scope of the problem; (b) current efforts and innovative approaches; (c) measures for improving the transition.

In the case of the first two of the above topical subheadings, information is displayed in country-by-country synthesis. Chapter 2, 'Nature and Scope of the Problem', provides, in addition to listing the ten most commonly found problems, a brief country-by-country synthesis of the most important problems faced in dealing with the transition from technical and vocational schools to work. Chapter 3, likewise, provides country-by-country synthesis. In this case, the summaries are more extensive and treat four subtopics in some depth for each reporting country. Chapter 4, 'Measures for Improving the Transition', is a more general treatment, with occasional country references or citations. Seven subtopics are reviewed which represent areas of promise for improving the transition. Finally, a brief chapter of conclusions is offered.

The subject of this report – and of the symposium, the country reports, and other related documents – is among the most critical of those facing educators, researchers, planners, administrators, officials of industry and business, and government officials today: the transition from technical and vocational schools to work. While there is considerable variety among nations as to specific problems and their causes and possible solutions, it can be stated with certainty that the problem of transition from school to work is a pervasive global concern with far-reaching economic and social consequences. Demographics, social values, economics and geography all contribute to the complexity of the issue. These factors vary considerably among nations. Yet there are several common areas of concern and interest, some having the appearance of being completely mutual among otherwise different and diverse nations. It is in these areas of mutuality that there may be promise for multilateral solutions. It is worth while here to strengthen this point by repeating five of the most significant results of the symposium discussions.

As reported in the initial summary of symposium discussions (Appendix 3), there was general consensus on the following:

The general education and training process of a nation has great influence on the importance and role of the technical-vocational education process and system. To be truly effective, technical-vocational education must be conceived of and practised as an integral part of the overall education system of a country.

Lack of qualified teaching and guidance staff and a concommitant problem problem of inadequate in-service training programmes or facilities for technical teachers exacerbates other structural and organizational problems related to the school to work transition.

The attraction of students to vocational and technical education programmes of schools is clearly a world-wide and transition-related problem. Lack of early exploration of the work site by young students and weak guidance and counselling programmes are important contributing factors.

Special populations of current and potential workers, including women and young girls, migrant workers, the physically and mentally handicapped and those with language limitations represent a visible international problem related both to generic technical-vocational education as well as to transition from schooling to work.

New attention is necessary with respect to the importance of the basic learning skills – reading, writing and communication, and factoring with numbers – as fundamental learning blocks upon which good vocational-technical education should be based. This is often referred to as the 'vocationalization' of general education.

The transition from technical and vocational schools to work

These five statements represent only a few of the issues, sub-problems and related concerns which affect, either directly or indirectly, how educators, governments, parents, students, employers, industry and business and communities – or entire nations – will deal with the problem of transition from school to work over the next ten years or more. It is to be hoped that this report, and the symposium and country reports which it aims to summarize, will offer a few answers – and, perhaps more important, some new and valuable ideas – which will contribute to the progressive resolution of this pervasive, international problem.

2 Nature and scope of the problem

The diversity in social and economic conditions among the various countries, as well as differences in their education and training systems, tends to exacerbate the problem of identifying, with clarity and precision, the nature and scope of the problem of transition from technical and vocational schools to work. Of the several topics considered in this report, none is more eclectic than this. The variables are many, but not endless. Commonality of problems, while rare, may be seen as significant, particularly with respect to multilateral solutions to problems experienced by member states.

In the most basic sense, it is necessary to consider technical and vocational education as an integrated system, comprising all programmes which aim at the development, in appropriate environments, of cognitive and practical skills (Appendix 3). It is within the context and sense of that statement, plus the specific country reports, the Revised Recommendation (Appendix 1) and the initial summary of the symposium (Appendix 3), that the substance of this chapter is provided. No attempt is made to compare one country with another. Each brief summary is intended to highlight what the country had to say about its particular and often unique problems related to the transition from technical and vocational schools to work. Only those countries which chose to outline specific or general problems of the school-to-work transition are reported. The treatment of each is intentionally brief. It is clear that countries are far more concerned with solving problems than with a lengthy listing of them. Still, without this exposé, the nature and content of the issue of problems would be left wanting. It is with that in mind – appropriate and realistic context – that the summaries are offered.

While significantly different and unique problems do exist from country to country, it is possible to summarize at least ten problem areas which are common to virtually all the reporting countries. Because this listing represents problems found in a distinct majority of reporting countries, the problem items appear to be strong candidates for broad and multilateral resolution actions.

Lack of sufficient guidance and counselling services for students of technical and vocational education programmes was the most frequently cited weakness. Few countries had full-time and/or properly trained guidance counsellors or guidance teachers. Compounding factors include: lack of training facilities for these staff; strong competition from industry for their services; unrealistic

caseloads of students; and inadequate substitution for unavailable counsellors by regular teachers – or even other students – who have had no formal instruction in counselling.
- All countries agree that increasing levels of technology at the work-place have led to greater demand for technically trained workers – today's students. There are, however, different needs in terms of numbers of workers and particular occupational skills required, depending upon the level of technology within the given country.
- There remains a certain negative stigma attached to vocational-technical education; academic orientation usually carries more prestige and status as far as students, parents and others are concerned. Several countries note progress in this area, however.
- Many countries harbour a concern that excessive emphasis on vocational and technical development will leave students weak and lacking in general studies and theoretical capabilities.
- Apprenticeship programmes, often cited as a strength area, still suffer in many countries from lack of appropriate work-places and qualified supervision.
- While several countries report recent positive efforts in the area of development and implementation of manpower surveys, the reliability of such undertakings continues to leave most nations without accurate and useful data/information for predicting future economic trends, future job markets and the skills needed for the jobs of tomorrow.
- Nearly all countries agree that better integration of education and skill training with the business and industrial sectors is needed.
- Job placement services are generally and uniformly lacking, and their rate of success is rarely high. While there are a few bright spots in a few countries, there are no indications of functioning, nation-wide systems of job placement.
- Location of vocational education and training centres is uneven (not enough in urban areas or isolated rural locations, for example) even though recent efforts by some countries to locate facilities near both jobs and population centres seem to be working.
- There is a stated and universal need for more effective teacher and counsellor training and retraining, especially at the industrial site. A companion problem, with respect to improvement of programmes and systems, is the general lack of sufficient emphasis on research and curriculum development.

Problems specific to each country are summarized following.

Algeria

This country is currently experiencing a significant imbalance between labour supply – especially technically trained workers – and demand. Severe underqualification of the employable population is noted. Some 90 per cent do not achieve a high-school diploma. There is also a general shortage of teachers for all subjects, not only vocational and technical. As to manpower planning, there is not sufficient consideration at the central planning level, and current surveys on the capacity of the education and training system to receive and train students are noted as superficial and imprecise. A new philosophy of the relationship between education, training and jobs is reported to be emerging and is suggested as an important step in resolving these and other problems.

Australia

Four principal problems inhibiting the transition are noted: a high ratio of students to teachers; clarification of the meaning of 'transition' and further exploration of the stages, problems and elements of transition from school to work; improvement of student motivation, both in terms of attracting students to technical-vocational programmes and maintaining their enrolment therein; and distance from school centres and the wide dispersal of the population. This country also needs additional resources for research, curriculum development and the improvement of career information systems for students, teachers and counsellors. Little if any vocational or occupational study is introduced before the upper secondary level, although options for student choice exist in many educational settings. Australia also reports a problem of linking the various levels of schooling internally – from primary through secondary to post-secondary.

Barbados

Among the problems cited is the fact that there are no institutions for technical and vocational education other than secondary schools, and the expense of providing technical-vocational education is a serious and limiting factor. The country is experiencing high unemployment. Linkages between schools and the business-industrial sector are difficult even though the establishment of an 'employment service' has helped somewhat. Insufficient co-ordination of out-of-school programmes with work-sites is noted, as is the general lack of good co-ordination between in-school programmes and the world of work. More available and more accurate information on vocational-technical occupational opportunities is needed. Work programmes are limited in availability at the secondary schooling level, but are more accessible at the tertiary level. New procedures for follow-up systems of graduates are being established, although at present this system is considered a weakness.

Democratic People's Republic of Korea

In 1945, this country had a national illiteracy rate of 80 per cent. The nation found itself with virtually no technicians, little industrial equipment and few workers to operate it, and other problems of language, availability of training institutes and the concomitant problems of recruiting and training effective technical and vocational teachers. Illiteracy was wiped out very quickly and the country is committed to maintaining a strong programme of general education so as not to allow technical education to dominate to the point of narrowing the desired broad educational and cultural base. As it continues to gain industrial and economic strength, this country will rely increasingly upon a highly skilled and trained work-force, and is currently planning for the most effective possible systems which will help to solve problems before they become more severe.

Ethiopia

While there has been a recent significant increase in the availability of technical and vocational programmes, the country has experienced important problems in initiating and implementing this movement. The problems of developing new and different curricula, establishing an apprenticeship system and recruiting and training teachers and counsellors are among several cited. The country sees a great need to establish a centre to provide comprehensive information on technical and vocational education, and is at present studying the viability of establishing a national commission for technical and vocational education. Competition between education and industry for available and qualified personnel as teachers and counsellors poses a major problem.

German Democratic Republic

The German Democratic Republic currently faces a serious undersupply of skilled workers and reports a very low level of unemployment, bordering on nearly total employment, in its current population available for work. The country is committed to raising the level of vocational training and employs the apprenticeship scheme extensively to this end. One important problem reported is that many work-places do not fully utilize their workers' capabilities and qualifications, thus contributing to considerable job changing among some groups of skilled workers. The country is continuing its efforts to raise the image of technical and vocational education in the esteem of the public, with some reported success in recent years.

Federal Republic of Germany

With its 'dual system' of education and training and the requirement that all students attend vocational school part-time and in parallel with on-the-job training, the Federal Republic of Germany still faces some important problems in solving difficulties experienced by students in making the transition from school to work. The present and lengthy system of evaluation could be made more efficient, it is reported, if specially trained teachers at vocational schools worked with vocational counsellors, rather than the counsellors visiting the schools over extended periods. Many students (a reported majority) who complete training courses do not find jobs which offer them further training opportunities and thus tend to settle for unskilled work. Moreover, those who drop out from the schooling system do not avail themselves of the training that is available for them. Many prospective new workers (trainees) do not currently give financial considerations a high priority in their choice of an occupation; for example there is an excess of unoccupied training places in the building trades sector despite the high level of trainee allowance (payment). There are also particularly problems in dealing with the handicapped population. A useful definition of 'handicapped' is thought to be needed and greater parental support (both financial and moral) is sought.

India

Unlike general education, there has not yet evolved a rational organizational structure for technical and vocational education in India. The country is dealing with the problem of reducing the undesirable effects of uncontrolled admissions to universities in the face of rising graduate unemployment. Polytechnic institutions are reported to 'have become autonomous of their partnerships with industries,' whilst at the same time they provide inadequate programmes to update workers through refresher courses. The integration of technical and vocational education with general education curricula is reported as a special problem. Also, India reports a lack of facilities to train technical-vocational teachers, an absence of guidance clinics, career courses and employment information, and essentially no long-term market predictions for particular jobs. The latter problem tends to result in students choosing occupations on the basis of current job status and not of trends in the overall labour market. While there is no lack of academic teachers for the schools, the system is forced to engage part-time instructors and teachers from industry for vocational instruction.

Iraq

The rapid economic development now taking place in Iraq (due in part to the nationalization of the oil industry) has major ramifications for technical and vocational education and for the transition from school to work. Effective guidance and counselling is a continuing problem in that there are no separate guidance teachers and no quantitative indicators of effectiveness of the guidance counsellors who do exist. There is a reported loss of teaching specialists from the technical-vocational system to the industries, which is partly solved by hiring part-time teachers from industry and by increasing the practical training of students at industrial sites. The increasing demand for more workers with higher levels of technical skills is seen as a continuing challenge, and one which will carry with it certain transitional problems.

Nigeria

This developing nation cites a severe shortage of technical teaching staff at all levels of technical education. Part-time teachers from industries are utilized, especially for teaching of evening programmes. Placement is not seen as a particular problem at this time owing to the low supply level of technically trained manpower and the high demand. Many technically trained workers tend to choose so-called 'white-collar' work where pay is higher and working conditions generally more attractive, thus widening the gap between availability of and demand for trained technical workers. In one effort to correct this situation, administrators plan to expand on-the-job training for students so that they can have an earlier introduction to the work-place and thus secure better and more realistic information and experiences upon which to base their decision of an occupation. Follow-up activities on graduates of technical and vocational programmes are reported as insufficient, although corrective steps are under way.

Senegal

The predominant problem area reported by Senegal concerns co-ordinating vocational-technical programmes under one overall policy. At present there is a high level of diversity of both purpose and administrative approach among several sectors, both public and private, which offer or want to offer and control technical training. The desire to unite training measures within a common national policy and under one administrative-governance organism is evident in the country report. Attention was also given to the particular problems of training young girls and women for specialized employment.

Sudan

This developing nation is currently experiencing a shortage of trained manpower. No technical or vocational exploration, preparation or training is offered at the primary or intermediate levels of schooling, even though few students proceed beyond those levels to any form of higher education. The majority of students completing intermediate levels of education either enter the workforce directly or find themselves unemployed – or worse, unemployable. Technical education begins at the secondary level, and is populated primarily by students who fail to find opportunity in the academic schools. Currently, theoretical subjects are emphasized at the rate of nearly 70 per cent of the curriculum, and where the vocational shops do exist, they are often found to be poorly equipped, with inadequately trained teachers. Relationships between technical secondary education and the socio-economic needs of the country fall at present far short of those needed for a strong delivery system. Only modest integration exists between and among the various training activities. Responsibility for planning and implementation of training centres is scattered among different government agencies and private establishments.

Sweden

This country, which reports few critical problems regarding the transition from technical and vocational schools to work, is currently emphasizing the improvement of contacts with industry and trade unions. This effort is intended to make education, particularly technical and vocational education, more relevant to employment. The fact that this country reports few changes in the technical and vocational education and training system in recent years is seen as an indication of limited problems with regard to the transition topic.

Thailand

The lack of any official linkages at the national level between technical and vocational education and industry is noted as an important problem. However, this country is extending efforts to create such linkages at the local level, which is seen as a method for causing more relevance to be brought to the instructional curriculum. At the moment, no true work-study or co-operative work-education programme exists on a significant scale. Teacher quality and improved in-service training for teachers are seen as important needs. As with almost all reporting countries, guidance and counselling is singled out as a problem of significance, although full-time guidance teachers are the norm. Where there is a shortage in this area, another teacher with some background in the guidance and counselling area may be recruited for part-time service.

Union of Soviet Socialist Republics

While the country report of the Soviet Union details few, if any, specific problems, the emphasis in certain areas of vocational-technical programme development can be seen as a continuing effort to deal with the specialized problem of transition from technical and vocational schools to work.

The emphasis on basic and applied research in the vocational-technical field has produced important results for dealing with the transition issue. The one-year, five-year and long-term planning processes also take into acocunt the special requirements of students and enterprises regarding the school-to-work transition. The content of training programmes, work-study arrangements and strong emphasis on instructor training are signal efforts to deal with and solve problems before they become too difficult and surface as obstacles to a smooth transition from technical training to the work-place.

United States of America

While considered by many in the United States to be the most effective mechanism for accommodating a smooth transition from school to work, the co-operative work experience programme continues to suffer from certain problems. There is difficulty in finding enough suitable work-places, competent supervision both from the school and at the work-place is not always available and co-ordination between education and employers in general is not at a desirable level. Accessibility to vocational education in large, urban centres and in isolated rural areas is a problem of critical national significance. There is a notable imbalance of available facilities for technical and vocational education between the suburban areas/medium-sized cities and the central city/very rural locations. Equal education opportunity through vocational education for women, minorities, the poor and the handicapped continue to exist as critical and visible problems, although progress is being made in each of these areas. Greater involvement of private business and industry persons is also needed for guidance and counselling programmes and as well as in the field of advising on appropriate and up-to-date instructional curriculum content.

3 Current efforts and innovative approaches

Countries undertaking the enormous task of reorienting, restructuring and expanding their education systems to meet the problems of transition from technical and vocational schools to work are devoting more in-depth attention to the role of technical and vocational education within their broader education system.

From the country reports under study, the symposium discussion summary, the draft basic working document and the Revised Recommendation, it is evident that the participating countries recognize the problem of transition from school to work and have, in fact, generated some productive, responsive current efforts and innovative approaches to address this problem.

Several recurring approaches to solving the problem were stated; some consensus of opinion by countries was reached. The following were indicative of these areas of interest:

The necessity for a comprehensive and continuing educational and vocational guidance system was highlighted.

Visits to two guidance centres in the host country provided interesting and useful field experiences.

The importance of preparation of guidance counsellors and development of information systems about occupations and job opportunities (as well as placement services) was noted as critical.

The organization of different types of technical and vocational education and training was discussed.

Apprenticeship programmes and co-operative work experience programmes were focal points of discussion. The importance of research in developing new methods of training (such as the modular approach) was referred to by several participants.

The organization of polytechnical education and subsequent vocational training was reviewed.

Participants agreed that the two visits to organizational structures (one group visited an industrial enterprise in Hemmingsdorf and the second group visited an agricultural co-operative in Malchin) were beneficial.

The importance of co-ordination between education and training and production and employment at all levels of policy, planning and execution (implementation) was underlined.

Furthermore, a consensus exists as to the objectives of technical and vocational education in relation to the total educational process, which may be summarized as follows; it is in accordance with the Revised Recommendations:[1]

6. Given the necessity for new relationships between education, working life, and the community as a whole, technical and vocational education should exist as a part of a system of lifelong education adapted to the needs of each particular country. This system should be directed to:
   (a) abolishing barriers between levels and areas of education, between education and employment and between school and society; . . .
   (b) improving the quality of life by permitting the individual to expand his intellectual horizons and to acquire and to constantly improve professional skills and knowledge while allowing society to utilize the fruits of economic and technological change for the general welfare.
7. Technical and vocational education should begin with a broad basic vocational education, thus facilitating horizontal and vertical articulation within the education system and between school and employment thus contributing to the elimination of all forms of discrimination.

This chapter will serve to review, synthesize and analyse each country's current efforts and innovative approaches to the problems of transition from technical and vocational schools to work. To facilitate that end, the organizational structure for each country summary will identify four topic areas (current organizational structure, current content and methods efforts, teaching staff and innovative approaches) and present related sub-topics in each topic area that will better focus each country's efforts to address the problem. This structure will be:

Current organizational efforts: manpower surveys; industrial co-ordination; work-study arrangements, apprenticeships, co-operative programmes, placement, educational employment; physical placement of schools; follow-up system of graduates; new administrative arrangements, industrial training boards, technical and vocational councils, sponsoring systems, evaluation systems.

Current content and methods efforts: new methods; vocational guidance; curriculum development; integrating theory and practice; research.

Teaching staff: separate guidance teachers; part-time industry teachers; co-ordination of teachers – transition.

Innovative approaches: new approaches.

Thus, this structure will summarize both the results of the symposium itself and related relevant methodologies employed by the participating member countries.

---

1. See Section II, 'Technical and Vocational Education in Relation to the Educational Process: Objectives', of the Revised Recommendation concerning technical and vocational education, pp. 78–8.

Algeria

Current organizational efforts

Algeria is committed to solving the problems of transition from technical and vocational schools to work. National planning and manpower surveys are conducted to facilitate the productive utilization of human resources in conjunction with direct economic needs. The manpower survey carried out by the Ministry of Town and Country Planning (Board of Statistics) concerns the number of persons in training at the end of each year and establishes statistics according to the ministry responsible for training, type of institution and level. Industrial co-ordination and placement in the world of work is effected by employment services under the auspices of the Ministry of Labour and Vocational Training. Algeria's philosophy of work-study arrangements concentrates on the adaptation of education/training to jobs.

Current content and methods efforts

Educational and vocational guidance is important when solving the transitional problems from school to work in Algeria. At present, information and guidance for youth is essentially effected in educational and vocational guidance centres (*centres d'orientation scolaire et professionelle* (CSOP)) falling under the responsibility of the Ministry of Education. Annual guidance-updating surveys are carried out on the education training systems' capacity to receive and educate students both by educational and vocational guidance centres of the Ministry of Education and by the Ministry of Town and Country Planning. The Ministry of Labour and Vocational Training has given the employment services responsibility in this information and guidance role.

Curricula are being expanded to meet the economic requirements of the country. Polytechnical education is committed to the conveyance of the values of technological aspects of humanism and the realization of an education integrating theory and practice.

Teaching staff

Algeria recognizes the need for and is seeking to facilitate the enhancement of linkages between teachers/trainers and employers of skilled manpower.

Innovative approaches

Algeria has identified and implemented several innovative approaches to solve the problems of transition from technical and vocational schools to work. Educational organization reform has given rise to a new type of school in Algeria: the nine-year school. This reform combined the three years of lower-secondary education with the six years of primary education preceding it to result in a nine-year basic education with a technical orientation.

Algeria is bringing the employment services and CSOP closer together. This move is intended to facilitate complete and precise information on training and employment openings.

Other innovative approaches foreseen in the present system include the launching of exceptional and massive activities in the field of out-of-school training, notably correspondence courses, scholastic recovery courses and apprenticeship.

Finally, Algeria is anticipating better linkages between technical and vocational institutes and industry. This would facilitate the articulation of industrial human resource needs and required skills and the offerings of vocational education programmes. Building fundamental polytechnic schools constitutes one of the measures to achieve this end.

Australia

Current organizational efforts

One organizational effort utilized in Australia to facilitate transition is manpower surveys. Although manpower surveys do not dominate planning for technical and vocational education, they represent an area that Australia recognizes for development. The basic institution-industry co-ordination mechanism is the college council. The powers of these councils provide them with a major role in linking the local community with the college. Most colleges also engage in industrial liaison through the release of some teachers for short periods and by involving people from industry in short course development. At state and territory levels, the co-ordinating mechanisms involve advisory committees and state councils. These include appropriate people from all professions, including the employment sector. The functions of these councils include curriculum review and development, facility construction and publicity. The criterion normally directing the placement of schools is the presence of a population large enough to make an institution viable, not necessarily an area with local employment possibilities. Since most technical and further education students enrol in part-time programmes, work-study arrangements are not an integral part of the course. However, it is usually expected that students will be employed in the areas in which they are trained. Apprenticeships are a good example. Apprenticeship training is normally co-ordinated by bodies such as industrial training commission apprenticeship boards. These promote the concept of apprenticeship, arrange contracts of employment (after the would-be apprentice has found an employer) and oversee in a general way the apprentice's training and progress. Limited follow-up studies have been conducted on graduates across the educational spectrum. However, individual colleges often follow up graduates on a minor scale and use the information to modify programmes, promote these programmes in other institutions, and promote programmes in the employment sector.

Current content and methods efforts

Vocational guidance is an integral part of individual training programmes at the upper secondary level and in transition programmes. Most vocational guidance is given on an informal basis by the teachers. Some systems have a central guidance resource, such as Victoria's Vocational Orientation Centre. The major change leading to more relevant curricula is the introduction and implementation of increasingly sophisticated curriculum models and curriculum planning. Although complex in nature, planning is essentially becoming more systematic and consistent. Certain states have adopted particular models similar to those used in the armed services in both Australia and overseas, adapting them to their needs.

Teaching staff

Many secondary schools through Australia have careers guidance teachers appointed on a full-time basis; most others nominate a teacher to act as a careers guidance officer on a part-time basis. These people are invariably teachers with considerable experience and have often worked outside the teaching service. Normally they do not have formal guidance qualifications although most have attended in-service training programmes designed to increase their competence in this area.

One of the major aims of technical and vocational education is to provide relevant training by people who know their job. To this end, large numbers of teachers from industry are appointed on short-term contracts as part-time teachers. Teacher training is carried out in tertiary institutions, either universities or colleges of advanced education.

Innovative approaches

Two initiatives begun in 1980 are designed to reduce the inefficiency of the independent efforts of the country's research and development efforts. First, a National Technical and Further Education (TAFE) Centre for Research and Development was established to analyse the skills required for various occupations and to review and evaluate TAFE curricula. The second initiative is the development of a National Research Clearinghouse for the collection and dissemination of information on research and related activities in TAFE.

Australia has initiated a variety of transition programmes. Since 1977, these programmes have burgeoned so that now there are link programmes, pre-vocational programmes, foundation courses, transition classes and educational programmes for unemployed youth. These are often developed locally, or at least modified locally, so that the curriculum is more relevant to the needs of the participants and to the local employment context. Teaching and learning strategies for these programmes have generally moved some distance from traditional methods, with far greater attention being placed on the needs of the individual, which means smaller groups, semi-structured as well as structured programmes and physical separation from regular school or college premises. Studies so far completed show that such strategies are very promising, although the management and general administration of the effort is undergoing improvement.

Barbados

Current organizational efforts

Barbados is working to solve the problems of transition it has encountered between the technical and vocational schools and the work environment of students/graduates. Manpower surveys are one organizational effort that assists in this endeavor. The government has commissioned the Barbados Institute of Management and Productivity (BIMAP) to secure objective data on which to base decisions relating to manpower requirements and, hence, educational plans and provisions. BIMAP is contracted to: (a) conduct an ongoing analysis of trends in technical manpower demands at all levels; (b) provide estimates and projections in such detail as to enable direct relationships with formal and non-formal training and educational outputs; (c) provide assistance in the design and analysis of longitudinal-type tracer surveys for relevant cohorts; and (d) assist with institutionalization of systems and procedures for the ongoing performance of the aforementioned three provisions.

Surveys of a more limited nature are also conducted on a periodic basis by the Ministry of Labour, the Statistical Services and the Chamber of Commerce and the results are fed into technical and vocational education programmes. Co-ordinating mechanisms between technical and vocational institutions and industry exist in Barbados. The Ministry of Education plays a key role in co-ordination, in the context of the formal education system. Representatives from commerce and industry sit on boards and committees of technical and vocational institutions. These advisory committees also assist in the co-ordination efforts. The National Training Board also plays a key role in the co-ordinating mechanism. Specific functions of the Board are to: (a) ensure an adequate supply of trained manpower in occupations in Barbados; (b) improve the quality and efficiency of occupational training for apprentices and trainees; (c) regulate trade test administration and certification of trade efficiency to competent candidates; (d) protect and promote the welfare of apprentices and trainees; (e) ensure that the operating costs of apprenticeship and other occupational training are distributed equally among employers; (f) arbitrate if and when differences arise between apprentices or trainees and employers; (g) perform such other functions relating to apprenticeship and other training as may be prescribed.

Work-study arrangements in Barbados include apprenticeships and other co-operative programmes for students in the vocational and technical training programmes. Due to the compact size of Barbados (430 square kilometres), no technical or vocational institution is more than 45 minutes away by bus for students. However, most of the technical and vocational institutes are located where most of the employment opportunities exist. Although actual follow-up systems after graduation are not routinely utilized in Barbados, the need is recognized and steps are being taken to implement such a system. Guidance teachers in some polytechnic and community colleges are establishing such follow-up systems.

Current content and methods efforts

Vocational guidance has been traditionally offered in most institutions offering technical and vocational education and training in an *ad hoc* and informal manner. In some secondary schools, fairly comprehensive guidance programmes have been established which involve the use of materials, resource persons outside the school, visits and tours to places outside the school and discussions and formalized sessions directed at guiding and counselling students.

To facilitate proper co-ordination of curriculum reform, the National Curriculum Development Council was inaugurated. It was charged with the total evaluation of existing syllabus and study programmes in the system, determining whether such contents were adequate or in need of revision and determining new areas of study and orientations to be introduced. New curricula in almost every subject area have been produced and field tested. Current research activities in the area of making graduates of technical and vocational schools more employable have been of limited scope but are being expanded and made more systematic.

Teaching staff

Concerning guidance teachers, Barbados is in the process of setting up comprehensive and systematic guidance services and guidance teacher education. Qualified skilled and experienced craftsmen are often employed part time to instruct students in schools and other institutions providing technical and vocational education.

Innovative approaches

Innovation concerning guidance is being undertaken. A vocational guidance officer was appointed by the government and based at the Ministry of Education. His duties include assisting guidance teachers and formulating programmes in guidance. The government is also working to provide a teacher of guidance in each government school. Within the last ten years, the Ministry of Labour and Community Service has established services in the area of youth guidance and counselling.

A second innovative approach to facilitate the transition from technical and vocational schools to work is the Skills Training Programme. The Skills Training Programme is organized through the Ministry of Labour and Community Services and is intended for young persons (between the ages of 16 and 25 years) who are unemployed. Proceeding through modular training, the programme provides the trainee with the basic tools for self-employment. Each training module lasts approximately three months – five eight-hour days per week for twelve weeks. Relevant elements of the community are involved at every stage (industry, manufacturers, youth groups, etc.).

Democratic People's Republic of Korea

Current organizational efforts

This country's education system has made significant strides in technical education since national liberation in 1945; prior to then, not a single college and only a few vocational technical schools existed. Since that time, the Democratic People's Republic of Korea has addressed its educational concerns and attempted to solve the problems of transition from school to work. In the Democratic People's Republic of Korea, the state directs planning that concerns balance of trades, scale of training skilled workers and manpower surveys. Co-ordination of education and industry is facilitated through correspondence and evening courses taught at factory colleges and through highly specialized institutes at large factories and enterprises. (In 1972, the factory higher-technical school developed into the factory high-specialized institute.) The work-study arrangement involves the studying-while-working-education system, parallel to the full-time educational system and expanding the number of daytime colleges. Vocational schools are not set up in every factory and enterprise, but rather in the factories and enterprises with extensive experience in training skilled workers and in those with a comparatively large reserve of new workers. These factories and enterprises also train workers of the same trades from neighbouring factories and enterprises. The creation of a comprehensive cadre-training centre in every province is of significance in overcoming the dependency on the central institutions for national cadres. These local institutions help to meet the local demand for technicians and specialists, both in quality and quantity, to promote local economy and culture.

Current content and methods efforts

The People's Democratic Republic of Korea has also made significant strides concerning current content and methods to facilitate the transition from technical and vocational schools to work. A five-year plan of curriculum updating and economic analysis is utilized to closely co-ordinate technical education and the development requirements of the national economy. One national philosophy concerning current efforts sees a need for all of the country's youth to acquire more than one kind of technical skill and to master the techniques and knowledge necessary for carrying out tasks assigned to them. Furthermore, the policy of closely combining class practice with productive practice during the whole period of technical education is maintained at the stage of common education.

Teaching staff

Teaching is one of the highly regarded professions in this culture and thus has received considerable attention. Every province has its own agricultural, medical, normal and teachers' colleges. In the higher technical schools, technical personnel are trained to assume the role both of technician and of skilled worker with the completion of secondary education. All teachers of technical education at the secondary level are educated at technical colleges. These colleges have special technical departments for teacher training. The guidance for skill training during the productive practice period is provided mainly by technical teachers and competent high-ranking skilled workers.

Innovative approaches

Two specific innovative approaches are apparent. Since 1972, universal compulsory education was instituted. It consists of a one-year compulsory pre-school education and a ten-year school education. This universal eleven-year free compulsory education extends through secondary education until students reach the working age. Students in the colleges and higher specialized institutes receive scholarships and their living expenses are paid, including clothing and text books at low prices. The eleven-year compulsory education does not provide vocational training before the end of secondary education nor does it divide secondary education into two courses, humanity and natural science. Much emphasis has also been placed on adult educational opportunities. The People's Democratic Republic of Korea is now endeavoring to provide adults with the knowledge corresponding to the senior middle school course and, as mentioned earlier, more than one technical skill.

A second innovative effort is the concept of establishing practice shop and practice work-team systems for the experience of the students. Factories and enterprises near schools provide students with these model working-condition environments and equipment. At these shops, students practise production techniques under the guidance of technicians and able skilled workers. These products of student efforts are utilized within the education system. For example, in the practice workshops of electro-technical schools, students design and produce simple experimental apparatus such as ampere meters and volt meters or such complex machines as an oscillograph and an electric computer. Through the course of inventing, designing and producing educational equipment necessary for the schools, students make practical use of acquired knowledge and skills.

Ethiopia

Current organizational efforts

Ethiopia has recognized the problems of transition from school to work and is taking steps to solving some of those problems. Manpower surveys are conducted at the national level by the Planning Department. This department's main function is planning and programming material facilities for the smooth execution of the education programmes. It has full responsibility for exploiting the internal as well as the external means and possibilities in line with national planning and programming. Industrial co-ordination with education is one of the responsibilities of the National Council for Technical and Vocational Education and Training. The council is entrusted with the powers to co-ordinate and issue directives, and promote guidelines governing technical and vocational education and training in the country. The council is not only responsible for the co-ordination of in-school and out-of-school (in-plant) training programmes, but also for ensuring that linkages are made between training and industry and the necessary skills and performances needed in the world of work. Members of the council include individuals from industrial and business communities, government ministries, agencies and service organizations, and independent training institutions. The council's main activities include:

To ensure that the training programmes are designed to serve the requirements of rural development.

To reduce and eventually eliminate wasted trained manpower and unnecessary duplication of training programmes among training institutions.

To ensure the quality and standard of training programmes and curriculum geared to meet the needs of the country.

To set standards of training for all levels of training programmes and institutions.

To determine standards and procedures of certification and accreditation.

Regarding general manpower training, the country has at present numerous educational institutions at all educational levels geared to the training of skilled manpower for the country's economy. The major training institutions are Agricultural Colleges, Business Colleges, Commercial Schools, Polytechnics, Technical Teachers Education Institutions, Schools of Medicine, Engineering Colleges, etc. All of the above institutions train to meet the need of high-level manpower. The middle-level manpower is trained in technical and vocational schools run by the Ministry of Education.

Basic training programmes are also conducted by organizations such as Ethiopian Airlines, Electric Light and Power Authority, Telecommunications, Ethiopia Roads Authority, Commercial Bank, etc. These companies prefer to conduct their own training because they cannot afford to hire people who have already had the necessary training.

To facilitate the transition from technical and vocational schools to work, goals have been established by the National Revolutionary Development Campaign (NRDC) to implement production targets in industry, agriculture and other economic branches. Ethiopia has determined that the implementation of these targets strongly depends on the different levels of skilled manpower, the level of training and the needs of the country.

Apprenticeship is another concept that is receiving wide acceptance in the education system. Although apprenticeship is in its infant stage in industrial plants, it appears to be the most efficient method of developing specific skills.

Ethiopia has implemented several new organizational efforts to address educational needs. They are:

Continuing Education. The programme is provided for school leavers and for skilled and semi-skilled workers who joined the labour force and wish to acquire further practical knowledge for upgrading skills and improving their performance.

Community skill training centres (for rural adults). The programme is involved in the developmental work of the locality in question.

Work-place education (production, distribution and services). The programme is offered by the concerned agencies for employees in out-of-work hours to upgrade job skills and productivity for particular industrial jobs.

Correspondence education. The programme envisages upgrading courses for all levels in urban and rural areas wherever the communications means exists.

Current content and methods efforts

Curriculum has been updated in technical and vocational education to be current with industry and business requirements for employment. The curriculum is being geared to integrate class work with field work so that students after graduation can handle their assignments with minimum guidance from their employers. This curriculum updating is being reflected in the technical and vocational schools as well as the comprehensive high schools.

Sample schools have been established to implement instructional materials and determine whether they represent or reflect the concrete condition of Ethiopia and meet the comprehension levels of students. Research and experimentation are also conducted in the sample schools.

Regarding contents and methods, Ethiopia has four major fields of specialization in vocational education. They are: (a) production technology; (b) agriculture; (c) home economics; (d) commerce and economics.

The integration of theory and practice is given serious consideration in Ethiopia. From 50 to 60 per cent of the school schedule is allotted to practical work and the remaining 40 to 50 per cent to theory.

Teaching staff

Prospective teachers are trained in the teacher education departments at the various institutions. Among these institutions, some offer methodology in addition to the pure subject matter and some, depending on the nature of their specific responsibility, teach only the technical and vocational subjects. Industrial representatives or individuals from other related enterprises are utilized in instructional programmes for teachers.

To meet teachers' needs for professional guidance and/or educational information related to their specific discipline, the Awraja Pedagogical Centres develop training materials that serve as models for teacher-developed instructional materials and also serve as feed-back centres for both the national and local curriculum by collecting evaluation data from the schools in the awraja.

Innovative approaches

Labour education is one newly introduced innovative concept in Ethiopia. It is one of the mechanisms to be employed in facilitating the transition of technical and vocational schools to work. In labour education, students will work up to six hours a week, without interfering with the normal class schedule. The programme contains services, agriculture, road and building construction, maintenance and participation in the literacy campaign. Governmental organizations co-operate and participate in the programme. Thus, the national level in Ethiopia is involved in solving the transitional problems from school to work.

France
Current organizational efforts
France is taking steps to facilitate solving the problems of transition from school to work. Current organizational efforts include manpower surveys conducted by the Centre d'Etudes et de Recherches sur les Qualifications (CEREQ). This public institute analyses and makes specialized forecasts on occupational qualifications and their evolution and searches for linkages between the functioning of the education system and the evolution of the employment situation. Co-ordination mechanisms between technical and vocational institutions and industry exist at various organizational levels. These arrangements facilitate dialogue between the state, employers' organizations, workers, consular offices, chambers of commerce, chambers of agriculture, family organizations and educational representatives. At the national level, dialogue is ensured by occupational consultative commissions. These are made up of three equal groups of representatives of public powers, of employers and of workers (having occupations under the competency of the commission), to which are joined experts (technological education advisers), representatives of educational personnel, students' parents, chambers of commerce and of occupations, etc. It is up to these commissions to define training, to specify its content and methods of control and to formulate an opinion on the consequences of forecasted needs. At the local level, regional and departmental committees for vocational training, for social upgrading and for employment have the task of measuring as accurately as possible the employment situation and perspectives and diverse systems of training, of adjusting the balance between these and of assuring the full use of proper methods and of becoming familiar with – and re-orienting if necessary – planning equipment. these local advisory committees, as advisers of technical education, participate in the examination juries, in diverse surveys (on the value of introducing a new type of training, on the functioning of private institutions, etc.), in the preparation of the scholastic plan, in assisting inspectors of technical education, in providing orientation information to first cycle students, and for certain advisers, in the inspection of apprenticeship. An interoccupational agreement provides for work-study arrangements to include educational institutions and workers in the industrial, commercial, craft and agricultural sectors. In addition, pre-vocational classes and classes preparing for apprenticeship exist that permit students of the required age – notably, those in the observation cycle who at the end of schooling, want to train for a particular occupation – to prepare themselves for the choice of a profession. At the conclusion of these courses, the students may either enter the world of employment or acquire vocational training by becoming apprentices either under an apprenticeship instructor or in an apprenticeship training centre, or enrol in a *lycée* for vocational education to

prepare for a vocational-skill certificate. The physical placement of schools is determined by the scholastic plan of public secondary education which takes into account geographic, demographic and economic data of the population. France's national graduation follow-up system is an exhaustive and permanent system which observes the entry into the world of work and follows the occupational itineraries taken by youth at the end of their initial education.

Current content and methods effects

France, too, is concerned with current contents and methods involved in transition. The guidance system is closely linked to the education system. Recent changes have been made to programmes and curricula to make them more relevant to employment. This renovation manifests itself in three directions: (a) creation of a pedagogy by objectives and of a continuous control of skills; (b) integration of training in industry with education; and (c) reform of the preparation for training skilled workers (Certificate of Vocational Skill).

Teaching staff

France has also utilized its guidance teachers as part of its teaching staff. Although there are no separate bodies of guidance teachers in France, all teachers contribute through their teaching, evaluation of student achievements and participation in student councils for the guidance of students. Licensed counsellors have completed two years of specialized training consisting of, on one hand, demography, economic sciences, sociology and social psychology, technology of professional activities (technology, knowledge of jobs, of professions and of training) and knowledge of institutions and legislation and, on the other hand, training-periods in industry (of one month's duration between the two years of training) and regular visits to enterprises.

Innovative approaches

Two innovative approaches should be cited in France. The first was the creation in 1970 of the Office National d'Information sur les Enseignements et les Professions (ONISEP). In conjunction with the concerned universities, administrations, professions and organizations, ONISEP's duty is to develop and put at users' disposal documentation necessary for information and guidance, to contribute to studies and research permitting the development of this documentation, to facilitate the process of information and guidance and to carry out studies and research improving knowledge of occupational activities and their evolution. Within this office, there is a centre for analysing jobs and professions, evaluating changes in qualifications due to the evolution of techniques and studying the adaptation of educational forms and methods to ascertained needs. This centre is at present proceeding with the setting-up of a French directory of available jobs and of a national organism to observe the paths young people take when passing out of the education system into the world of work.

A second and related innovation is the follow-up system for students after graduation or departure from the school system. To this end, the centre pilots the national organism which observes the transition from school to work, known as the 'National Observatory'. The observatory aims at being a device which: (a) provides a complete view of the entry into the world of work of trained youth (articulation between levels and general education and technical education, and inter-regional balances); and (b) describes, in a sufficiently refined and homogenous way, types of vocational education and occupational situations (specialty of training and of work, inter-regional comparisons).

The observatory, being a national organism, cannot systematically carry out analyses corresponding to limited geographical zones, but rather demonstrates the diversity of underlying local situations and their place in the official overall view of the national situation. This dimension, therefore, constitutes an important element of France's education-employment relationship.

German Democratic Republic

Current organizational efforts

The German Democratic Republic is attempting to solve the transitional problem from technical and vocational schools to work through vocational education. Vocational education comprises the vocational training of young people (vocational training of apprentices) and the training and further education of skilled workers and foremen (adult education). Manpower planning or central planning is conducted by the state. The planning of vocational training distinguishes between long-term planning (for a period of ten to fifteen years), five-year planning and annual planning. The various levels of planning include central planning by the state, regional planning and enterprise or manpower planning. The Council of Ministers of the German Democratic Republic is responsible for central planning by the state. It decides on basic issues of the development of vocational training, and regulates responsibilities. The planning bodies of the regional authorities (county and district councils) use economic information and decisions as a basis for analysing the number of school leavers for vocational education and other related issues. Enterprise planning is concerned with the development of the economic community and training facilities. Manpower surveys are conducted. These analyses of vocational conditions direct student occupational choices. The lists of apprenticeships which are annually issued by the district councils for the subsequent year of training serve as a direct orientation for the forthcoming choice of a vocation. Apprenticeships are utilized as work-study arrangements; they enable an apprentice to practise an occupation in at least one complex sphere of work. Apprenticeship training is supervised jointly by skilled workers and skilled worker-instructors. Enterprise vocational schools – state-controlled educational establishments attached to the industrial concerns and enterprises – train about 75 per cent of all apprentices. In addition there are factory-run vocational schools. The vocational school of the nationally owned district factory for agricultural technology is responsible for training young people from the country's fourteen districts as technicians for agricultural machinery.

For all vocations in which training opportunities are offered, there are special social bodies called vocational expert committees, or advisory committees. The members of these committees are professionals, vocational educators, economists, scientists, technicians, trade-union representatives and youth association members. The activities of the vocational expert committees are centred on vocational analyses and the elaboration of job descriptions and curricula on the basis of these analyses.

Current content and methods efforts

In the German Democratic Republic, the system of careers guidance is extensive. Careers guidance familiarizes both pupils and parents with the given social conditions under which individual professional objectives can be realized. The 217 careers guidance centres in the country disseminate this information. Over 90 per cent of the pedagogical staff of these centres are university, college or technical school graduates. Building upon this solid qualification base is further education in the form of a two-year post-graduate course on careers guidance and cyclical advanced education provided for all careers advisors.

Vocational and technical education is intended to give a well-balanced theoretical and practical vocational training experience. The schools – which comprise a vocational school for theoretical instruction, the apprentice workshop or other facilities for practical vocational training, and an apprentices' hostel – are intended to guarantee the unity of vocational and ideological education throughout both the classroom and workshop periods.

Teaching staff

Teachers in the education system undergo further training and updating of skills. Every year 10 per cent are delegated to attend advanced courses. All are engaged in further training courses (methodical commissions).

Innovative approaches

A major innovative approach is that of youth projects. These youth projects consist of concrete, assessable tasks in economic areas of prime importance – be it on an enterprise level or on a national level – which are contained in the long-term and annual plans. Such youth projects are taken over by youth teams under the leadership of the Free German Youth. The majority of members of such a youth team are young workers who are assisted by a few experienced skilled workers. Irrespective of their work tasks, the young skilled workers increasingly develop a sense of responsibility towards work and society. More than half of them are prepared to co-operate as representatives of their work teams in committees and bodies which have been set up in the enterprises themselves, or in popular representative bodies.

The transition from technical and vocational schools to work

Federal Republic of Germany
Current organizational efforts
Educational planning in the Federal Republic of Germany is based on the social demand approach and not on the manpower requirements approach. One organizational measure undertaken by the Federal Republic of Germany is that of co-operative work experience education or the dual system. Young people in the Federal Republic of Germany obtain their occupational training according to the dual system, called thus since occupational training proceeds parallel on the job and at school. Occupational training programmes and apprenticeships are used in the country's work-study arrangements. As a rule the training period of a youth will last three years. The trainee receives a monthly trainee's salary which increases over time as skills increase. The training salary is governed by trade-union agreements. In fields where the production programme is highly specialized, it is sometimes not possible to cover the entire scope of the training content. In these cases, training shops maintained by several employers supplement the occupational training programme. The training phase terminates with a final examination which is held by the specific chambers (chambers of industry and commerce, chambers of agriculture, etc.). This examination determines the success of the training programme, and, at the same time, certifies the occupational qualifications of a skilled technician, a clerk or a journeyman (craftsman).

The Federal Institute for Vocational Training was established to promote the number of vocational training locations. The main institutions of vocational training and education are those responsible for training and education in the 'dual system', the companies and the vocational schools. The procedure is as follows: the companies decide on the number of training places to offer; the unions have rights of co-determination in the planning and practice of vocational training in companies and in training administration; legislation for company training is at the federal level and the federal government is responsible for rulings on the contents of training courses, public recognition of occupations and other matters related to vocational training. The Federal Republic of Germany also promotes in-plant training and grants vocational training subsidies or allowances to student participants, based on financial need. Retraining displaced workers is a consideration, although the percentage of displaced workers is small.

Current content and methods efforts
Vocational guidance and counselling is a focal point in the Federal Republic of Germany. Vocational counselling has the purpose and function of helping people to help themselves. The vocational counselling service also has a legal basis for the provision of an all-comprehensive information and counselling system for vocational training institutions and facilities. While practical occupational training takes place predominately on the job, theoretical occupational training and general education are centred in vocational schools which all young people must attend until they are 18 years of age. The Federal Institute for Vocational

Training is involved in considerable research for vocational and technical education.

Teaching staff

All members of the Federal Employment Institute staff are regularly required to attend courses and seminars of further training which are held in the Institute's own adminstrative schools. They are also required to participate in various series of lectures given on an on-duty basis, and to occasionally spend terms of practical on-the-job training in the industry. Even the executives, such as department and section chiefs, are regularly called upon to attend further presentations for study and training.

Innovative approaches

A major innovation is the effective utilization of the country's vocational guidance and counselling services. The practical work of vocational counselling is incumbent upon and performed by the local employment offices. For this purpose each employment area has a separate department for vocational counselling. To some extent these specialized vocational counsellors are organized in a so-called base network system, which means that they are responsible and work for several local employment offices. The eventual placement in vocational training or apprenticeships is handled by training placement officers in most of the local employment offices.

A second innovative approach of the Federal Republic of Germany is the establishment of the Federal Employment Institute. This institute promotes institutions or establishments that provide vocational training facilities or programmes. This promotion also includes the granting of loans for the erection of dormitories or homes for the accommodation of the trainees or apprentices, as well as the granting of subsidies and loans for the construction of general vocational training centres. These investments by the private or public organizations for the practical implementation of basic occupational training courses are designed to improve the chances of integration for young people who could not or cannot find a place for vocational training or apprenticeship.

India

Current organizational efforts

A large-scale attempt to reconstruct education to solve the transitional problems from school to work has been undertaken in India. The Planning Commission handles macro-level manpower planning with a view to proposing measures for the optimum utilization of human resources for development. Manpower surveys are also conducted to identify employment trends and to estimate the need for facilities in relation to projected industry requirements. To facilitate transition to work, integration with development planning is needed. A smooth transition from education to work is sought by establishing durable links between the educational policy and the employment policy, on the one hand, and between educational development with employment objectives in the development plan particularly as articulated in the proposed investment patterns for the different economic and industrial growth sectors. One type of work-study arrangement employed in India is the concept of apprenticeship. Employers are obliged in specified industries to engage apprentices in accordance with prescribed ratios in the trades designated for that purpose. Apprenticeships vary in length from six months to four years and entry qualifications range from five to eleven years of schooling, depending upon the trade involved. Apprenticeship consists of basic training followed by on-the-job or shop-floor training with related instruction throughout the period of training. In addition, technical representatives are encouraged to participate in the boards of management/advisory councils of technical institutes.

Current content and methods efforts

Curriculum development centres are established in selected institutions such as the technical teacher-training institutes for polytechnic education and the National/State Council of Educational Research and Training. Curriculum research follows a systems approach to curriculum design, development, implementation and evaluation; these are distinct stages and elements of a feedback loop of the process. Research has determined the need for managerial/entrepreneurial skills for small industries and self-employment; elements of relevant management education are now included in technical education. The National Council for Training in Vocational Trades is responsible for facilitating the integration of theory and practice. This council was established in the Ministry of Labour and Employment to arrange trade tests and to award national trade certificates to those who successfully complete the course.

Teaching staff

To accommodate regional needs for teacher education, four technical teacher-training institutes and six central training institutes for training instructors have been established. These institutes attempt to develop subject matter competence, teaching ability and orientation towards industry among potential teachers for polytechnics. They also hold short-term in-service courses and seminar/workshops for senior faculty members and institutional administrators in curriculum development, on the management of human resources, industry-institutional co-operation in technical education and local resource generation. In-service guidance training and regular courses are organized for training college teachers to acquaint them with information collection procedures and cumulative record sheet maintenance. Norms and designs of tests of intelligence, aptitude and personality are also developed.

Innovative approaches

India has identified several innovative approaches to solving the transitional problems from school to work. The first is to be found in the development of the

Draft Five-Year Plan, 1978–83. This plan, the foundation of educational policy and its articulation through developmental programmes, is the responsibility of the Ministry of Education at the national level and the state departments of education. All these agencies are represented in the Central Advisory Board of Education and the All-India Council for Technical Education, the highest level policy advisory bodies in the field of education. The Draft Five-Year Plan 1978–83 called for radical changes in the education system, particularly for greater vocationalization, through co-ordinated action and quality improvement rather than proliferation of secondary and university education facilities.

A second innovative approach involves vocational education in higher secondary schools. The Ministry of Education is playing a leading role by financing district vocational surveys to identify course outlines and, through the National Council of Educational Research and Training (NCERT), to prepare suitable guidelines for curricular patterns and designs.

A third approach deals with the guidance aspect of vocational and technical education, a development of the University Employment Information and Guidance Bureau which is functioning in sixty-six universities. This organization collects, compiles and disseminates occupational information for the use of students, teachers, parents and jobseekers, both individually and in groups. Career talks, group discussions, career exhibitions and film shows are arranged. Assistance is also rendered in securing apprenticeship training opportunities and in placement, particularly during vacations and on a part-time basis.

Another approach is the development of sandwich courses. Attempts have been made to organize technician education on a sandwich pattern, alternating the students between institutions and work places according to a well-designed plan. This effort seeks to integrate classroom work with practical experience in a real world environment, thus moulding the attitudes of students towards the rhythm and rigor of working in industry. It is intended to enhance students' self-realization and direction, their appreciation of the conditions of work in the enterprise where they are placed and, at the same time, provide the employing organization with an opportunity to identify its potential employee manpower and train it in the most appropriate manner, given operational requirements.

Another innovative approach is the emergence of industrial training institutes. The main objective of this type of training is to ensure a steady supply of skilled workers for industry. In order to enhance acceptance by employers, training is confined to one specific trade in which necessary manipulative skills of prescribed grades are sought. Generally, practical work accounts for over 50 per cent of total student time. This is, in essence, a parallel development (extensive training programmes of craftsmen) to that of the vocational system. Initially established during the Second World War, it was recently reintroduced.

Iraq

Current organizational efforts

Since the nationalization of the oil industry in Iraq in 1972, there has been an increased demand for technical skills at all levels. Thus Iraq is interested in solving the school-to-work transition problems. Detailed manpower surveys are conducted. Industry and education are being co-ordinated. Representatives from industry sit on the advisory councils of each technical institute and, in some cases, instructional department. All students train in industry for various periods during their course of study, under joint school, institute and industry supervision. Work-study arrangements include employees from various industrial establishments attending evening classes, taking the same certifying examinations as vocational school students. Students must complete a minimum of twelve weeks of summer training in industry or related establishments before graduation in order to fulfil the co-operative educational employment criteria.

The distribution of vocational schools and technical institutes throughout the country was made on the basis of population density, type of economy in the area, industries established or planned for the region and student population and growth. A fair geographic distribution of schools and technical institutes has been maintained and the proximity of industrial establishments was considered in the physical placement of such schools. This facilitates easy out-of-school training.

To obtain good feedback on the external efficiency of technical education, the Foundation of Technical Institutes introduced in 1978 a 'tracer' system of follow-up for graduates. The quality and relevance of the curriculum are measured by the questionnaire as well as the type of employment graduates are obtaining.

Current content and methods efforts

Vocational guidance is entrusted to the teaching staff of vocational schools and technical institutes. The students are divided into small groups and assigned to a teacher who meets with them regularly to monitor their academic and educational progress. During the summer, all students are required to spend six weeks in supervised training in industry where they familiarize themselves with the type of employment they will be offered after graduation. Visits are also organized during the year to a number of related establishments. In some cases, students spend two or three days a week training in nearby establishments as part of their course work.

Curriculum is constantly being updated to meet economic requirements for employment. The curriculum for vocational education emphasizes practical training and applied subjects, representing a total of 60 per cent of the curriculum. Summer training for all students in related establishments is an integral part of the curriculum.

Teaching staff

A guidance committee is set up in each institute to direct guidance activities.

Although there are no separate guidance teachers in schools at the present time, vocational teachers do direct the guidance programmes.

Many lecturers from industrial and other establishments are employed by the vocational schools and technical institutes. These instructors maintain links between schools and industries and jointly supervise the practical training of students in industry.

Teachers are encouraged to keep up to date with technological advances. The staff of the institutes are obliged to spend a minimum of six months in industry every five years in order to gain academic promotion.

Innovative approaches

Several innovative approaches are being employed by Iraq. One is the extensive utilization of manpower planning. Clear, effective economic planning for all sectors of the national economy is being facilitated by the manpower planning. Educational planning, as an integral part of manpower planning, has been developed to meet the changing needs of a society with a rapidly developing economy. Manpower plans concurrent with the five-year national economic plans identify the needs of each type of specialization at different levels of skill. First priority is given to vocational and technical education in particular, and manpower development in general. Major plans for building schools and technical institutes have been formulated and implemented.

A second development is the introduction of industrial arts into the intermediate secondary-school curriculum. Also, some experimental secondary comprehensive schools have been started.

Other innovations undertaken by Iraq are the: (a) proposed expansion of technical institutes; (b) increased staff recruitment and training; (c) qualitative development of technical education; (d) expansion of parallel technical education (secondary-school graduates working in industry or other sectors are trained through courses organized in co-operation between the Foundation of Technical Institute and the relevant establishment to become technicians in their field of specialization).

Nigeria

Current organizational efforts

Nigeria is interested in solving problems of transition from technical and vocational schools to work. The Ministry of National Planning and Development is conducting manpower surveys and determining their impact on technical and vocational education. The purpose of these manpower surveys to collate data on manpower requirements for national development and educational projections. Nigeria employs the apprenticeship scheme which is a form of work-study arrangements. One type of work-study involves company-sponsored training schools for company purposes. Another scheme of co-operative programmes/apprenticeship is the Student Industrial Work Experience Scheme (SIWES) which provides the opportunity for some students in selected fields to be given industrial work experience for a three-month period each year. Regarding the physical placement of schools, with the exception of a few experimental institutions, most technical institutions are located in areas of higher employment possibilities. Nigeria recognizes the need for a follow-up system for graduates and is currently revamping early attempts to fill this need.

The National Board for Technical Education (NBTE) involves industries and institutions by setting up subject panels of experts or advisory councils. In addition, NBTE is responsible for restructuring courses from time to time for purposes of certification and accreditation.

Current content and methods efforts

Educational guidance is still in its infancy in Nigeria but it has been tapped for expansion. Career guidance counsellors attend seminars to upgrade skills. A programme exists for progressive in-service training to fully qualify as education officers or school teachers as guidance professionals at federal and state levels. Many institutions are now preparing brochures for prospective students on career possibilities in various fields, outlining the basic requirements for entry to those courses. A few experimental institutions test technical and vocational methodologies and curriculum. Curriculum development for all levels of technical education comes under the aegis of NBTE. Industry, since it is an element of the education system and must be convinced that products of educational institutions will meet its needs, is directly involved in curriculum development.

Teaching staff

Due to the general shortage of teaching staff at all levels of technical education, Nigeria secures personnel from industry as part-time teachers or lecturers in institutions. Industrial teachers generally instruct in the evening courses only, as industry has not as yet allowed daytime release of its personnel for teaching purposes. In all areas where there are planned industrial linkages, technical teachers participate fully in the supervision of students in industrial settings. This affords direct contact with employers and facilitates institution/industry cooperation. Nigeria is concerned with technical teacher training and has provided for teacher education. Teachers can prepare either to teach technical subjects in junior secondary schools as part of a general course or teach at technical colleges, colleges of technology and polytechnics with advanced pedagogical training. In addition, some of the polytechnics and colleges of education run an advanced three-year programme for technical teachers where the admission is based on successful completion of secondary education in appropriate subjects.

Innovative approaches

Nigeria's primary innovative approach to solving the problems of school to work transition is found in the Industrial Training Fund. For a long time the private sector tended to place low premium on skill training and manpower development, despite the fact that recruitment difficulties and deficiencies among existing personnel could be considerably reduced by a well-programmed training effort. A comprehensive and well-articulated skilled manpower training scheme related to the needs of the economy is important. Thus, the Industrial Training Fund was established to promote and encourage the acquisition of skills in industry or commerce with a view to generating a pool of indigenously-trained manpower sufficient to meet the needs of the economy. Financed jointly by subsidies from the government and contributions from employers, the fund's training activities include: (a) compilation of directories – providing information on a national level regarding training programmes, facilities, training institutions and training requirements: (b) training evaluations – determining effectiveness of training programmes against predetermined requirements and the fund's policy; (c) company survey programme – providing spot-training advisory services to member establishments, particularly those not engaged in training programmes; and (d) seminars for contributing establishments – generally two-day seminars acquainting contributors of services and activities of the fund.

The fund is interested also in vocational improvement centres and technicians, and financially supports evening courses at technical colleges and polytechnics. It also supports the Student Industrial Work-Experience Scheme (SIWES), a programme whereby students in institutions of higher learning receive training in industry or commerce compatible with their area of study. Finally, the fund conducts train-the-trainer workshops designed for foremen, chargemen, supervisors and instructors in industries, to sharpen their awareness as trainers.

Senegal

Current organizational efforts

Among other necessary actions, evaluations of manpower requirements are undertaken by Senegal to assist in educational planning. Expansion of the manpower survey process to include the whole of Senegal, region by region, is now being implemented. Industrial co-ordination is facilitated by representatives from the world of work who serve on a permanent basis as counsellors between education and the main sectors of the country's economy. Apprenticeship programmes are one means Senegal is using to implement work-study arrangements. Co-operative programmes constitute another action utilized to interspace full-time training with actual world of work experiences. Regarding the physical placement of schools and training, while Senegal's past practice involved saturating localities with schools and training, at present education expansion is restricted to those areas whose need is greatest. Although public funds are allocated to follow-up studies for students, expansion is needed for verifying training effectiveness and actual student placement.

Senegal has implemented some new administrative arrangements to facilitate technical and vocational education. New educational structuring concerning technical colleges and vocational education institutions is under way, focusing on integrating vocational training on a full-time basis and expanding sandwich training (apprenticeship) and continuing education. This reorganization is intended to enhance student possibilities for passing from one level to another through the integration of all types of continuing education, on either a full- or part-time basis.

Current content and methods efforts

Vocational and education guidance for students and curriculum development are important vocational education programme elements. The curricula used in technical colleges are continually updated. In math-related disciplines in particular, content requirements are being updated and standards raised. Technical and vocational curriculum is updated in conjunction with industry advances and needs. Co-ordination with education and industry is evident. Integration of theory and practice is accomplished in Senegal via sandwich training which provides the student with an apprenticeship contract. Terms of a contract for private work (three-year apprenticeship contract) state that the main body of the practical training is given within the firm itself. The rest of the theoretical and general training is handled via the vocational training institutions. Research is another current method being utilized. The Directorate of Research and Planning co-ordinates efforts to promote a better balance between technical and vocational training and employment needs.

Teaching staff

Senegal has concentrated its efforts on the training and development of technical and vocational teachers. A teacher-training college for technical and vocational education has been created. Training periods involve teachers for short-term vocational education, technical and secondary-education teachers, advisers and psychologists (vocational and educational guidance staff) and supervisory personnel. A department was also created for each professional sector to conduct research and provide pedagogical support. Current training programmes are carried out in consultation with higher education authorities and, more especially, in collaboration with the higher institute of technology.

Innovative approaches

Senegal has identified and implemented several innovative approaches to solve the problems of transition from technical and vocational schools to work. One of the more important is the continuing education programme, which provides students with optional full- or part-time study, training during working hours or through evening classes. This allows students to obtain vocational qualifications or to pass from one level of qualification to another. Further, provisions have been made for special institution 'open days' when workers, technicians, employers and craftsmen can bring to the students updated knowledge and information related to the development of techniques in their occupations. Furthermore, the National Vocational Training Centre is being restructured, in association with various institutes, to provide all regions in Senegal with facilities affording an opportunity to prepare professional qualifying examinations.

Another innovative measure recently implemented by Senegal is the creation of six permanent subcommittees responsible for adapting curricula and diplomas to meet new organizational restructuring demands. These subcommittees will study the following components for each type and level of training: adaptation of contents to employment needs; corresponding levels of training; recruitment levels; time-tables and curricula; continuous supervision of knowledge; and sandwich training and apprenticeships.

Sudan

Current organizational efforts

Sudan is, like other countries, concerned with solving the problems of transition from the technical and vocational schools to work. Records concerning the number of students involved with technical education is reflected in Sudan's six-year educational plan. Work-study arrangements in vocational training are supervised by the Department of Labour. Vocational training has two aspects: apprenticeship and skill upgrading.

Current content and methods efforts

A major focus of the current approach is the co-ordination of the responsibility of planning and implementation of training centres and courses. Sudan has also recognized the importance of integrating theory and practice and has implemented this philosophy. The training received by students in the mechanical, electrical and building trades is about 80 per cent practical, hands-on and about 20 per cent theoretical. It is believed that this qualifies students better to go directly to work.

Teaching staff

A significant effort is being exerted in the field of teacher training in Sudan. A large number of those who join the teaching profession depend on acquiring experience in teaching and developing that experience by practice and training under the guidance and direction of the Ministry of Education through its training institutes. However, at present, most teachers are trained abroad.

Innovative approaches

In that Sudan is a developing country, several innovative approaches to solving school-to-work transitional problems are being employed. Since at present there is no common system for regulating and keeping track of vocational preparation and training centres and courses, efforts are being made in that direction. Attempts are also being made to establish a national system of vocational training and apprenticeship. At present there are three main types of vocational preparation and training:
1. The youth centres established by the Youth Administration which accept

students who complete their primary education. Students in these centres receive a general craft preparation without any limit to specific trades.
2. The national handicraft centres under the supervision of the Ministry of Education which accept students who complete intermediate schools. They offer their students some training in national handicrafts relevant to the community environment where the centres are located.
3. The vocational training centres run by the Department of Labour which used to accept students who completed intermediate schools; they now accept only students who pass the intermediate certificate. This new criterion was the direct result of the Apprenticeship and Vocational Training Act of 1974.

The National Council for Apprenticeship and Vocational Training was established to provide consistent national trade standards for vocational training. At present, the vocational training centres of the Department of Labour and the training centre of the Mechanical Transport Department are the two delivery systems with standards consistent to the national trade standards established by the council.

A second innovative approach is providing vocational training via apprenticeship and upgrading of skills. The duration of apprenticeship training is three years, two of institutional training followed by one of on-the-job training in the industry. There is a very high demand in the labour market for the graduates of apprenticeship centres; in fact, students are reserved for employment two or three months before graduation, and the management of each centre finds itself in a crucial position in distributing the graduates among employers.

As to the upgrading of skills, courses are organized in the Khartoum upgrading centre, in some of the apprenticeship centres and within the public enterprises which request these services. Ranging from two weeks to five months, these courses are directed toward the workers already employed in the public or private sector. In this way, Sudan addresses both the young population in need of vocational training and the adult population interested in upgrading their vocational training.

Sweden

Current organizational efforts

Sweden has undertaken several organizational measures to facilitate the transition from technical and vocational school to work. Manpower surveys are conducted which generate needed statistical information for considering questions and outcomes concerning education and work. Co-ordinating mechanisms exist in Sweden between technical and vocational education and industry. The joint consultation body for school and working life facilitates this co-ordination effort. The primary work-study arrangement utilized in Sweden is that of apprenticeships. Physical placement of schools is in areas with employment possibilities for students and graduates. The follow-up system of students after graduation in Sweden involves investigation concerning school-leavers from both the two-year and the four-year systems. The main variables are occupation, work and studies, transitions to university studies and questions initiated by employers/consumers. Research is conducted by the Central Bureau of Statistics (CBS).

Current content and methods efforts

Vocational guidance is an integral part of vocational and technical education both at the four-year upper-secondary school and the two-year upper-secondary school. There are two different compulsory components of vocational guidance included in the training programmes for students in four-year technical education. During the first two years of education, the component called school/practice utilizes vocational guidance in the school/workshop curriculum. During the summer vacation of the last two years, there is a compulsory twelve-week environment/practice included in the education programme. This part of the education is performed as industrial practice at local companies and factories. Guidance teachers assist with the necessary contacts between school and industry.

Although few curriculum changes have been initiated in recent years, Sweden is addressing the need to revamp technical and vocational education curricula. The National Board of Education (NBE) distributes publications called 'curriculum supplements' which identify curriculum concepts to be taught and give NBE directives on the implementation of their implementation. These curriculum supplements are continually updated.

Research into transition problems is also undertaken, oriented toward making graduates of vocational and technical schools more employable. Two research activities are: (a) in-depth research into the local education system and its relation to community and industry – the purpose is to describe the problems in a local school system with emphasis upon the relation between education, work and community life; and (b) in-depth research concerning vocational lines of upper secondary schools – the aim is to create a basis for future decisions about measures concerning the educational process, educational materials, vocational and medical-vocational guidance, basic education and in-service training for teachers.

Teaching staff

In Sweden there are separate guidance teachers working in the school system, usually one in each school. These teachers have a three-year education in special university branches for teachers' training. Normal entry requirements are three years of upper secondary school and one year of job experience, including at least six months continuous experience outside the education system.

Teachers from industry are also engaged in the technical and vocational institutes as instructors on a part-time basis, but only on a limited scale. In some communities technical teachers are involved to a considerable extent in co-ordination and co-operation between schools and employers. In certain subject areas tasks are involved where the student is to carry out special work, often in co-operation with industry. This activity is intended to engender closer relations between school and working life.

Innovative approaches

Three distinctive, innovative approaches are being utilized by Sweden in its attempt to solve transition problems. The first is the SSA committee, a co-ordinating mechanism for technical and vocational education. This joint consultation body for school and working life is the overall co-ordinating mechanism between technical and vocational institutions and industry. It deals with the compulsory comprehensive school as well as with the upper-secondary school. For two-year vocational schools especially, there are vocational committees, one for each of the main programmes, such as the building and construction programme, etc.

A second innovative approach is the sandwich course programmes. Some vocational programmes with a maximum duration of two years can be either full-time or sandwich courses. In sandwich courses, the student integrates classroom and work-related practice to complete the vocational programme.

Another approach deals with skill-upgrading of workers. There are experimental short-cycle technical-vocational courses. The study programmes are intended for industrial workers and prepare them for key advancement posts. To be admitted, a student must have undergone basic vocational training and have at least four years' working experience in his/her trade. Most programmes run for three terms. At present, programmes are directed toward the iron and steel, engineering, woodproducts, clothing, foodstuffs and paper and pulp industries.

Thailand

Current organizational efforts

Manpower surveys are regularly conducted in Thailand by the Department of Labour, the Guidance Service Centre and the National Statistical Office. Information collected includes manpower demands in a variety of occupations by levels of education. Furthermore, in each national economic and social development plan (which covers a five-year period), enrolment targets in vocational-technical institutions are specified in conjunction with projected manpower needs in that period. Although there is currently no official co-ordinating mechanisms between vocational-technical institutions and industry at the national level, efforts have been made by a majority of individual institutions to establish linkages with business and industry in their locality. For example, advisory committees consisting of representatives from business and industry as well as educational personnel and government officials are established for every institution. One function of the committees is to serve as linkages between the institution and industry in the community in securing or arranging work study or work experience programmes for students. In addition, placement of students upon graduation is facilitated and assigned by these committees.

No 'work-study' arrangements in the real sense of the word are conducted by institutions as a result of limitations of opportunities and availability of facilities in business and industry. However, vocational and technical institutions have always tried to provide direct work experiences for students. For example, students in business and office occupations may be placed in department stores or offices for up to eight hours a week per semester to gain the experiences required in their study programme. They may also receive minimum wages for their work. This kind of arrangement is encouraged and maintained by all institutions, especially those offering trade and industrial subjects. The schools are located in areas with employment possibilities for students and graduates. Every institution has a follow-up system which keeps records on employment status of its graduates. Generally the graduates are requested to inform the school about their employment situation approximately six months after graduation. Information is collected via staff-prepared questionnaires. The planning division of the Department of Vocational Education also maintains statistics on the employment status of students throughout the country. These statistics are collected from the schools and colleges and used primarily for guidance and planning purposes. While the existing follow-up system is currently thought to be far from perfect, it does provide management and administration of vocational-technical education with much-needed information.

Private vocational education is under government control. All schools and colleges below university level offering both formal and non-formal vocational education programmes come under the jurisdiction of the Office of Commission for Private Education. Fields of studies offered by these private institutions are similar to those provided by government schools and colleges. For example, formal three-year programmes normally include such courses as machine shop, electricity and electronics, and business administration. Non-formal programmes or short courses which usually last three to six months include hairdressing, typing and handicrafts.

Current content and methods efforts

Making school programmes relevant to employment is a major concern of the Department of Vocational Education. Vocational guidance is included in every school's programme. However, the nature and scope of services vary depending on local conditions. For example, institutions in large provinces or industrial areas usually have contact with business and industry and maintain effective placement services while those in rural areas may provide only needed information to students. Nevertheless, in most institutions cumulative records of students are maintained and educational and vocational counselling provided. Job sheets and operation sheets have been developed and utilized in almost every field of study. These institution sheets are based on job and task analyses of the occupations for which the students are trained. It is intended that students receive relevant experience and master skills necessary for jobs. Emphasis is placed on practical aspects of the training programme, with the intention that students acquire the experience and master the skills necessary for employment. The practical part of the curriculum of most schools now accounts for some 70 to 75 per cent of the total curriculum.

Teaching staff

In every school and college, guidance services are usually available to students. However, not every school can recruit a specially trained counsellor since newly-recruited guidance teachers are usually not willing to work in schools and colleges far from large cities. To alleviate the problem, many schools assign a teacher to work as a guidance teacher. This teacher is usually a college graduate, who has possibly taken a few courses in guidance and counselling techniques and who assumes the guidance workload on top of his/her teaching responsibilities. As far as possible, the Department of Vocational Education encourages schools to recruit qualified individuals from business and industry to conduct classes for students on a part-time basis. Teacher knowledge and teaching performance are enhanced through a variety of in-service training programmes. Teachers are allowed to further their education for advanced certificates and degrees in colleges and universities within the country and abroad. Those on leave to further their education receive full salary. They are also encouraged to participate in short training programmes regularly offered by institutes of higher education.

Innovative approaches

Several innovative approaches are being undertaken by Thailand. At present, the Centre for Vocational Education Training and Development is under construction; upon completion, it will be attached to the Supervisory Unit in the Department of Vocational Education. This centre will be responsible for conducting in-service training programmes for trade and industrial teachers. It will also engage in research and development activities.

Another innovation is the construction of area vocational centres, scheduled to open in 1981 and intended to serve out-of-school populations as well as secondary students who choose vocational courses as their electives. The programmes are geared to develop attitudes and skills as well as the knowledge necessary to enter gainful employment. They are designed in such a way that they can be transferred to and readily accepted by technical schools and colleges for further studies in technical education. They are intended to complement existing institutions, providing non-formal education programmes to a larger segment of the population.

Union of Soviet Socialist Republics

Current organizational efforts

Planning technical and vocational education and manpower surveys in the USSR are closely related. Every republic, region and district has plans for economic development and planning commissions responsible for the elaboration and execution of those plans. Technical and vocational programmes reflect these manpower plans. Programmes are compiled according to the requirements of skilled manpower. Enrolment plans are based on manpower demands of enterprises, ministries or departments, taking into account trade, profession and level of skill required, as well as the expected number of youths willing to acquire technical or vocational training. The USSR also practises both long-range and short-range planning in the form of one-year, five-year and long-term plans. Every five years, programmes undergo revisions which reflect scientific and technological development. Authorities of enterprises work with educational personnel to provide for proper articulation of industrial standards and education requirements. Students of vocational schools participate in industry work-study arrangements in enterprises, various establishments and institutions before their actual in-service industrial training, thereby giving them a chance to become acquainted with their future working places. During their actual in-service industrial training, students are taught not only the particular ways and methods of work, but also how to examine and solve technical, technological, organizational and economic problems created in the work process, as well as how to use technical guidebooks and manuals. A limited follow-up system of graduates is currently in existence in the USSR. Further, studies that have been conducted indicate that among vocationally trained workers there is less job leaving, a higher level of production efficiency and a better index of professional stability. Industrial co-ordination is accomplished in part by technical teachers who have higher education and teach special subjects. These teachers co-ordinate relations between institutions and workplace enterprises.

Current content and methods efforts

Concerning guidance, it should be mentioned that many teachers of special subjects guide students' work in special technical groups (teams) and promote their innovative and rationalization activities. These people contribute to the growth of students' professional skills, develop their technical mentality and prepare them for more successful work in their future career.

Development of practical and technological advanced curricula is a major focus in the USSR and is a strongly held principle regarding the integration of theory and practice. Industrial training now includes theoretical elements and theoretical education includes practical forms of work.

The Central All-Union Research Institute, in close co-operation with many industrial and agricultural research institutes and with the Scientific Research Institute of the Academy of Pedagogical Science of the USSR, deals with problems of technical and vocational education through various forms of research. A network of experimental schools for investigation and practical verification of theoretical propositions is at the disposal of the institutes. Scientific workers of methodological laboratories and educational establishments, along with scientific forces of all the Soviet Republics, are involved in investigating technical and vocational education problems, taking into consideration local peculiarities and conditions. Much of the research work is carried out in co-operation with higher education institutes and the Academy of Pedagogical Science of the USSR. There is also a Department of Vocational Pedagogy and Psychology at this academy along with the affiliated Technical and Vocational Pedagogy Research Institute which was founded in the city of Kazan.

Teaching staff

There is a broad and flexible network of teaching centres where technical teachers undergo special training according to their qualifications and specialities. They can take upgrading training courses in seventy industrial and pedagogical upper-secondary technical schools, choosing from among twenty-eight specialities (mechanical engineering, building/civil engineering, electronics, agriculture, etc.). The enrolment figures run to 19,000 teachers per year, including 4,000 who teach evening courses. Teacher training is also organized at higher technical schools. Specialists from basic enterprises are invited, if necessary, to teach technical teachers in order to keep them abreast with technology advances. In-service training for technical and vocational teachers to upgrade professional qualifications is also conducted, as is in-service training in technical and vocational schools for skilled workers already employed in order to upgrade their professional qualifications.

Innovative approaches

The USSR has identified and implemented a unique innovative approach in regard to the problem of transition from technical and vocational schools to work. That effort has been the co-ordination of relations between vocational schools and basic enterprises. Every vocational school is specialized in the training of skilled workers in a few particular trades and performs its duties on the basis of the so-called 'basic enterprise'.

The basic enterprises, establishments and organizations (one corresponding to each vocational school) are obliged, during the educational process as well as the industrial training period, to do the following:

Provide work/study arrangements.

Provide vocational schools with orders for goods, machine parts, equipment, etc. to be produced in school workshops and laboratories.

Provide vocational schools with information on scientific and technical achievements in the country and abroad, scientific research and development, and advanced experience in the field of personnel training, economics and organization of production.

During the period of industrial practice, provide students with special clothes, means of individual safety, special and remedial diets; make available housing and industrial rooms for students and teachers; provide work transportation.

Involve advanced working teams in the students' educational process; attract technical instructors and veteran workers for this purpose.

Ensure training of vocational school teachers in advanced workshops at the enterprise to refresh and upgrade their knowledge of modern techniques and technology and ways and methods of advanced working teams.

United States of America
Current organizational efforts

The United States is working toward solving the problems of transition from technical and vocational schools to work. Manpower surveys are carried out at both the national level via the National Occupational Information Co-ordinating Committee (NOICC) and at the state level via a system of state occupational information co-ordinating committees (SOICCs). NOICC is not a primary data collection agency, but is creating a structure for the inclusion of occupational supply and demand data for identifying occupational options for post-high-school education, secondary vocational training and individual career guidance. Basically, the occupational information system embodies all planning elements related to job training and job and labour market projections so that individual states may plan for their specific needs within the framework of a data collection and information system which can be aggregated at the national level.

There are several co-ordinating mechanisms between technical and vocational institutions and industry in the United States. Community involvement is assured through required national, state and local advisory councils composed of lay persons, business, industry and labour representatives and educators. In addition, the United States Department of Education is promoting and strengthening industry-education-labour (IEL) councils and activities in local, state and regional areas and providing information and data feedback on the effectiveness of these councils.

Work-study arrangements are also promoted. Co-operative education is an instructional strategy defined as the integration of classroom theory with practical experience under which students have periods of attendance at school and periods of employment. Apprenticeship programmes combine experience and training on the job with related supervised and theoretical instruction. Work-study programmes are also offered via vocational education. This work experience is not necessarily related to the students' field of study but is a form of financial aid to help the student remain in school.

Vocational school facilities are located primarily in large cities, suburbs of cities, small towns and most rural areas. However, adequate facilities and programmes are not found in abundance in some of the nation's largest urban areas. Follow-up systems are employed on a local basis for graduates with data aggregated at the state and national levels. While placement rates for students who complete technical and vocational education are respectable, the system for collecting such data is not yet fully effective.

Current content and methods efforts

Vocational guidance is included in training programmes, but better efforts are being made to provide consistency and availability of information to all students. In most institutions, trained guidance counsellors are accessible to students, but often vocational teachers serve this guidance function. Within the past decade, however, the federal government has initiated a major education and work movement known as 'career education'. The purpose of this movement is to provide occupational guidance and career information to individuals of all ages throughout the nation in an effort to increase their awareness.

Curriculum is undergoing major changes in the United States. There is a major shift to education based on demonstrated competence in both basic skills and job skills. The Vocational Technical Education Consortium of States (VTECS) was formed when sixteen states and two branches of the armed services joined together to develop curriculum guides based on performance objectives with criterion-referenced measures (worker responses). Other such consortiums have emerged in recent years.

Research is a major focal point for making graduates of vocational and technical schools more employable and easing the school to work transition. Research activities, conducted at all levels (local, state and federal), include:
A National Center for Research in Vocational Education with several mandated functions aimed at improving technical and vocational education across the nation.
Development of entrepreneurship training components for vocational education.
Industry-education-labour collaboration.
Basic skills development through vocational education.
Volunteers to improve vocational education in urban areas.
'Credentialing' women's life experiences.
The bilingual vocational oral proficiency test.
A model for awarding academic credit for work/life experience.
Curriculum development, revision and dissemination.
Research and demonstration projects.
Exemplary and innovative programmes.
Vocational education personnel development.
A National Occupational Information Co-ordinating Committee.

Teaching staff

Certified guidance counsellors, typically with a master's degree in a graduate counsellor education programme of a college or university, are employed in educational institutions to foster freedom and competency of educational and/or occupational choices of students. Personnel from industry are used both on a part-time and a limited-term, full-time basis, especially for vocational training purposes and increasingly for guidance team purposes. Teaching staff are encouraged, and in some cases required, to be involved in summer work experience as part of the periodic teacher certification renewal process. These experiences are often through a teacher education/co-operative education type arrangement. Vocational and technical teacher co-ordinators are extensively involved in co-ordination and co-operation between schools and employers. These professionals interact daily with employers, articulating business and community needs with vocational and technical education skills.

Teacher training for technical and vocational subjects is provided primarily through four-year colleges and universities. Increasingly in the United States, practitioners from the trades and crafts of business and industry are employed as full or part-time teachers, especially at the post-secondary school level.

Innovative approaches

The recent innovation Experience Based Career Education (EBCE) has considerable promise for the future. Initiated by the National Institute of Education and developed by four regional education research laboratories, it is a comprehensive community-based educational programme through which participants earn academic credit for basic skills and life skill competencies gained in a community setting. The EBCE experience features academically-focused non-paid short and long-term exploration. Students fulfil graduation requirements in English, science and mathematics as they interact with adult worker/mentors at job sites, such as newspaper offices, laboratories and computer firms. This effort portends a movement away from the strictly graded system, towards an achievement and work-oriented useful-living-skills model for learning.

Emphasis is also placed on building a work résumé, which provides the prospective employer with a useful reference for real work skills acquired in co-operative work experience or work-study experiences. Perhaps the most effective method utilized in the United States for improving the school-to-work transition is the co-operative work experience programme. Students, usually in their eleventh or twelfth year of education, work part-time for pay in an occupation related to the school vocational courses for which they are enrolled; attend regular academic and general courses part-time; and build a work résumé and establish contact with the real work world and with prospective employers.

Summary

Major efforts and innovations indicated by the documents and reports reviewed as a whole are summarized here. There remains a lot of detailed information in many of the specific country reports which interested persons may find useful.

Some concluding statements, however, aggregating the data which have related each country's current efforts and innovative approaches can be generated. To facilitate that end, this summary will follow the same organizational structure as that by which the country report summaries were reported.

Current organizational reports

Without exception, all countries identified some type of national planning or manpower survey system that directed or assisted the administration of educational planning generally, and technical and vocational programme planning specifically. Most countries have some form of industrial co-ordination with education concerning the function of vocational programmes. Advisory councils, at both the state and local levels, were most often cited as the co-ordinating mechanism. Some type of work-study arrangement was indicated by all countries; specifically apprenticeships or co-operative work experience were the most prevalent. A majority of countries report that the physical placement of schools was directly influenced by the high rate of employment opportunities that could be afforded to its students. Thus we find a majority of technical and vocational institutes located in large cities or highly industrial regions of the countries.

Only a small percentage of the countries expressed adequate satisfaction with their present graduate follow-up system. However, many countries had identified this need and were developing plans to implement an effective system.

On only a few occasions did a country cite a new administrative arrangement that was being employed to solve problems of transition. Industrial or trade training boards were those most often cited.

Current content and methods efforts

Vocational guidance was cited in all country reports as either fulfilling a vital function in the vocational programme or requiring content improvement so that it could fulfil that vital function. Major efforts in the area of curriculum development, reform and expansion were found in most country reports. The importance of guidance in the technical and vocational programme was unquestioned, though in some countries it was somewhat ignored and not kept up to date. Integration of theory and practice, although not specifically referred to in most country reports, was in evidence. Most instructional programmes were complemented with some type of work-study arrangement, showing evidence of the pragmatic application of the integration of theory and practice. Research was a subtopic rarely mentioned in the country reports, although some countries alluded to its importance in the future.

Teaching staff

In general, it can be concluded that vocational educators are trained professionals, often in short supply, and who rarely have opportunities to update their professional skills. A few of the reporting countries do encourage teacher skill updating via in-service training and release time for advanced degrees. Employment of part-time teachers from the trades and industry is not widespread, but all countries noted the value of this practice.

Innovative approaches

Without exception, all countries have developed at least one, and sometimes many, innovative approaches to the problems of transition from technical and vocational schools to work. A majority of countries identified programmes for improving vocational guidance and enriching counselling skills via programme expansions. A number of countries initiated transitional programmes or training efforts of some type to help the student who moves from the school environment into the work environment. Labour education was introduced by one country as an innovative approach. However, it is fair to conclude (and the consensus of all the reporting countries would be) that each country was advocating the introduction and implementation of some type of new programme or training effort that would specifically address the problems of transition from technical and vocational schools to work.

4 Measures for improving the transition

Several measures for improving the transition from technical and vocational schools to work can be found in the country reports as well as in the summary of discussion of the symposium.

Using the reports and the discussion as primary source documents, and with the Revised Recommendation and discussion outline as a framework, the measures for improving the transition can be grouped according to the following: (a) planning and policy development; (b) research, experimentation and information; (c) curriculum; (d) teacher and counsellor staff education; (e) guidance and counselling; (f) linkages with industry, business and commerce; (g) other specialized measures.

Where appropriate, references are made under each sub-topic to specific country efforts. Otherwise, summaries of central ideas and measures for improvement are drawn from the aggregate data of the country reports and the initial summary of symposium discussions (Appendix 3).

The Revised Recommendation (Appendix 1) provides guidance for framing several, if not all, of the sub-topics noted above. For example, Chapter V, paragraph 24, of the Revised Recommendation states in part:

Given disparities that may exist between formal education, whether secondary or tertiary, and the employment and career opportunitites available, the highest priority should be given to technical and vocational education which prepares young people to exercise occupations in the sectors covered by this recommendation. Consequently the structure and content of traditional education, whether general or technical and vocational, should be adapted accordingly through: (a) the diversification of secondary education in the later stages so that it may be pursued in conjunction with employment or training or may lead to employment or to higher education, thereby offering to all youth educational options corresponding to their needs;

This gives rise to the topics concerned with planning and policy development, curriculum and apprenticeship/co-operative work education. Chapter VII, paragraphs 54 to 59, provide direction for summarizing improvement measures in the area of guidance and counselling, while Chapter IX, paragraphs 72, 73, 77 and 84 guide the placement of teacher and counsellor staff among the topics of this chapter. For other sub-topics, general indications are found in the Revised Recommendation and more specific details in the several country reports and in the initial summary of symposium discussions.

Planning and policy development

In nearly every case, developing countries cite significant strides in recent years in the improvement of planning for vocational and technical education programmes. In those countries where planning and policy development are clearly and primarily functions of the central national government, such as in the People's Democratic Republic of Korea, the Sudan, Nigeria and Iraq, among others, comprehensive and systematic nationwide planning has contributed significantly to improvements in the integration of technical and vocational education into the general educational curriculum and has facilitated the transition of students from schools to the work-place. The same can be said for progress in more industrialized nations such as the German Democratic Republic and the USSR where central, national (federal) level planning guides the work of institutions and schools. For those countries with more decentralized education systems, such as Australia, the United States and the Federal Republic of Germany, progress in planning at the local and state (or regional less-than-federal jurisdiction) levels is also noted, although perhaps not to the extent as is reported by other nations. Local and decentralized planning and policy development tends to be made more complex, and possibly more difficult in terms of significant change and improvement, largely because of the far greater numbers of planning units and personnel involved. Often in these cases significant changes and progress is more difficult to measure at a specific timepoint since it tends to aggregate over longer periods. Still, it is fair to state that, with few exceptions, all countries involved in this topic – and the symposium itself – have reported both quantitative and qualitative advances in comprehensive and systematic planning. It is also noteworthy that neither the complexity nor the simplicity of the governance or organizational systems of the reporting countries deterred advances in the area of improved planning. This is to say that progress has occurred both because of, and often in spite of, bureaucratic designs that in other areas of concern might have dissuaded planners and policy-makers from taking necessary steps to improve local, state (regional) or national planning for technical and vocational education. This may be attributed to a new – or renewed – recognition of the important roles that technical and vocational education have to play in the strengthening of any country's social and economic situation.

Of the several topics contributing to improvement of the transition from technical and vocational schools to work, perhaps none is more profound in its impact than is planning. Interactions within the system of technical and vocational education do not occur by chance. They require specific, organized and systematic planning. Commitments of one sector (guidance and counselling, for example) to another (technical/vocational instructional programmes, apprenticeship systems, for example) have little meaning and less hope for achieving results if they are not articulated and connected in plans. With few if any exceptions, this notion is borne out in the actions of the countries reporting on the transition topic.

In the policy area, it is equally clear that the large majority of reporting countries has established, enlarged or improved policy bodies which focus specifically on technical and vocational programmes. In several cases, these entities are composed of representatives of several national-level government agencies (labour, education, commerce, etc.). Often, such committees, boards or councils have specific and broad powers for the generation of policy. There is, moreover, an apparent movement toward emphasizing the country's economic considerations when developing policy affecting training for work. While the values placed on the social and more general aspects of learning are usually preserved (and often given special emphasis), there is some indication in most of the country reports that the needs of the economy (as represented by the companies, businesses or enterprises) has a dominant effect on policy for technical and vocational education. The implementation or enlargement of the use of manpower surveys in virtually every reporting country is an indication of the shift in emphasis. In most cases, such surveys deal both with the availability (supply) of workers and the requirements (demand) of the work-place. The location of training facilities, the kinds of equipment put in place, the training of instructors and the placement of workers in specific occupations are all affected by the results of such surveys. Thus, by using factual and real-world information based essentially upon economic considerations, policy for technical and vocational training programmes increasingly reflects economic development needs in concert with the social, human and values requirements of a society or nation.

One particular aspect of both planning and policy development which received more attention in the symposium sessions than in many of the country reports is found in the area of special populations. The handicapped, migrant workers, the poor and women in the work-place emerged as issues of special concern during the multilateral discussion of the five-day meeting. The special problems of these populations are found in virtually every country reporting on this topic. For those students who suffer mental or physical limitations, there are problems at both the training and education end of the spectrum as well as at the work-place. The need for specialized teachers, curriculum and equipment further exacerbates their problems. As to the transition to work from schooling, for these students the process is often more difficult due to their impairments, lack of mobility and the physical restrictions of the work-place itself. In some countries recent policies have been put into place to give special attention to the handicapped. In the United States, for example, states are required to spend specific percentages of federal and state funds for vocational education programmes for the handicapped, and another set percentage for the economically and educationally disadvantaged. In many nations, special counsellors are provided for this population to assist them in making useful choices regarding technical and vocational training. In other countries, policies provide for the special equipping of laboratories and shops in schools or institutes for these students. Several nations are investing increasing funds in research and development aimed at the specific problems of educating and training for the handicapped.

The particular problems facing women engaged in technical and vocational education received emphasis in the symposium discussions and in some country reports. Interestingly, the nature of this sector of problems varies little among countries. Age-old patterns of bias and discrimination against working women appear to be nearly universal. For those women who are part of the work force, most are relegated to the lowest paying and most repetitive tasks. In many countries, the percentage of women in the work-force is growing, particularly in those nations with a shortage of workers, such as the German Democratic Republic. Greater attention is being given to the special problems faced by women, not only in education and training programmes but as they make the transition to the work-place, as well. Several of the reporting countries outlined recent policy steps which have been taken to assure the elimination of bias and discrimination against women in technical and vocational training programmes. Increased emphasis on appropriate guidance and counselling, better, more up-to-date occupational and career information systems on policy and planning councils, the presence of specialized consultants who are expert in women's education and training concerns and the required expenditure of specific amounts of funds to deal with women's issues are indicative of new efforts cited by reporting countries. Migrant workers' problems occupied a more restrained space than those of the handicapped or women. Certain developing nations, and a few of the industrialized nations which depend upon migrant workers to supplement their work force, reported particular problems in dealing with these persons. Often, the problem of language exacerbates other problems such as lack of training in a skill, transportation or adequate housing. There are also differences in the definition of migrant workers. What may be considered a migrant worker in one country (one who follows the harvests of agricultural crops, for example) may be quite different from imported workers (those from another country brought in specifically to supplement the work force of a country with short labour supply). In both cases, however, problems appear to be somewhat similar. The children of migrant workers seem to suffer most from a lack of consistent education and training. Their continuous movement about a country, as their parents follow work, places serious limits on their formal education and training. The workers themselves (parents, older brothers and sisters) frequently lack anything but the most basic of skills; they often cannot read or write in their native language. For the imported worker, again often considered a 'migrant', the lack of skill training may not be as serious inasmuch as such workers are usually imported precisely because they have skills needed by the host country. Still, they often face many of the same problems as the more typical migrant worker with respect to housing, transportation and continuing education and training. Policies of better planning and programming for the migrant worker population are emerging in some countries. The handicapped, women and migrants require special efforts in the planning and policy development arenas if both their needs and the economic requirements of the country are to be met. By all accounts, most of the reporting countries either have established such planning and policy elements or are sufficiently concerned with these groups to begin moving in a positive direction.

In general, the countries reporting on the topic of transition from technical and vocational schools to work and participating in the subject symposium have, individually and collectively, a strong and sharply developed sense of purpose with respect to the importance of comprehensive planning and responsive policy development in this field. It is perhaps even more important that each of these countries shows a commitment to policies which clarify and support the integration of technical and vocational education in the general schooling curriculum.

Research, experimentation and information

While few of the reporting countries indicate substantial investment or effort in the areas of research, experimentation and information, every country sees these areas as critical to the improvement of the transition from technical and vocational schools to work.

Probably the most extensive research-type effort is that associated with the conducting of manpower surveys. There is a significant movement in this direction among developing nations, and some major efforts to extend the surveying process in industrial nations are noted. While manpower survey techniques represent an inexact science at best – owing primarily to the diversity of information sources in most countries – such work appears to have important positive implications for improving the school to work transition. Manpower survey data have many uses in planning for new programmes, predicting needs for training in certain job sectors and, most importantly, providing the student-trainee or prospective apprentice with information for making an occupational choice.

There is general consensus that research in several areas (curriculum, teacher and counsellor training, utilization of workers from industry as technical teachers in schools, etc.) will ultimately contribute significantly to the identification of measures for improving the transition. Likewise, it is generally agreed that experimentation, based in part upon useful research, is needed in these same (and other) sectors in order to determine the true effectiveness of new or changing programme and training elements. At the same time, many countries complain that very limited funding is available for research and experimentation efforts.

Much the same can be said about information. An already diverse subject is made the more complex due to lack of clear definitions and identifications of the most important types and kinds of information needed, and by whom they are most needed. Most of the reporting countries see the issue of inadequate information tied closely to the guidance and counselling and planning processes. Without up-to-date and accurate information about jobs and work-places, guidance and counselling personnel can hardly be expected to deal with students adequately. It is these kinds of information – for students and parents who are in the choice and decision-making processes – that seem to be the most crucial and at the same time the most lacking in most countries. Data and information about job requirements, work-place environments, salaries and wages, education and training required and geographic location of jobs within a country appear to be most needed by young decision-makers and their parents or guardians.

Planners, too, require a wide array of information related to job availability, the effects of technological change on the work-place, curriculum and content improvement, supply of new and retrained workers, etc. Administrators at all levels of programme operation need information and data on these and other topics if they are to operate training and education programmes in the most efficient and effective manner.

Overall, the country reports and the symposium discussions strongly support the need for increased fiscal and human investment in research, experimentation and information systems development. In many cases, such undertakings may have implications beyond country borders. Opportunities may exist for joint and bilateral country efforts in such areas as information systems development and implementation, or for the study of the effectiveness of industry workers as technical teachers, for example. It is clear that most participating countries consider such investments as having implications for the improvement of the school to work transition.

Curriculum

There are few simple answers to solving the problems associated with maintaining contemporary curriculum for technical and vocational education. The central issue raised by virtually every reporting country was that of assuring that the school-based curriculum accurately reflects the reality of the work-place. Achieving that end can be a difficult task, particularly in those cases where linkages with business and industry are underdeveloped or even non-existent. There has occurred an apparent and considerable expansion in most of the reporting countries in the establishment of advisory groups, of one form or another, composed of persons who represent the industrial and business sectors. These groups are attached to technical schools, institutes and centres for the purpose of making recommendations to education personnel on improving curriculum, training or retraining teachers, selecting appropriate equipment, etc. They are also used as sources of current information on new developments resulting from new technology in the work-place. Such ventures hold promise for improving the transition. Their expansion and continuation was supported by most of the reporting countries.

Institutional arrangements, in colleges, universities and special national or regional research and development organizations also hold promise for curriculum improvement. It is through such centres that investments are made in the research, development and experimental pilot-testing of new curriculum inventions. Clearly, these efforts are tied closely to the research and experimentation topic discussed earlier. the assurance of additional resources for further work in the curriculum area through these institutions is a critical factor in both the short and longer terms. In times of fiscal restraint, it is often these kinds of higher risk ventures which are the first to suffer in the process of budget reductions. Yet, such efforts may be precisely the kinds of undertakings which will pay-off financially in the longer term. The foresight of administrative and policy decision-makers in such matters is not often as acute as their hindsight. This phenomenon appears not to be bound by country borders but is experienced in all nations, to one degree or another.

Teacher action in the curriculum improvement area is often found to be among the most fruitful of undertakings. This is particularly true when the teachers or instructors of technical and vocational subjects have had recent exposure to real world work-places. Teachers are typically early adopters of new ideas and methods, especially when they have observed the idea or method applied in a practical setting. Such practice ought to be encouraged by administrators and supervisors, and time for curriculum planning and development should be provided during the teacher's working day.

Adoption and adaptation of curriculum from other training sectors (military, private training establishments, industry-based training, for example) is progressing in some nations. The experiences of these other providers of technical and vocational education are often found to be rich resources for new content, improved instructional techniques and more accurate sequencing of training events. The expansion of 'competency-based' and individualized instructional content is also noted by certain countries. While not altogether a new invention in the curriculum and instructional domains, the competency-based approach seems to be catching on in several of the countries reporting on the transition topic. Because the method and approach are typically oriented to a self-paced paradigm on the part of the student, certain motivational factors are gained in concert with the acquisition of job-specific and site-specific skills and tasks. Some educators, however, are sceptical of the competency-based approach for they believe it to be too fixed in its routine to accommodate parallel development of the more affective and social skills also required of today's workers. Still, this approach is accepted as promising by many educators and technical trainers because of its flexibility, motivational values and the relative ease with which content updating can be implemented.

In sum, curriculum, with its many problems and facets, is considered by most of the reporting countries to be the key to unlocking doors which are often closed to the student in transition from schooling to the work-place. The measures concerning curriculum improvement could well be expanded and used to improve the transition from technical and vocational schools to work.

Teacher and counsellor staff education

As reported in other sections of this summary, this topic was the most thoroughly addressed in the country reports and among the most fully discussed at the symposium. Few of the participating member countries would deny that the teaching and counselling personnel – with their professional skills, personal attributes and dedication to their work – are the most influential of persons in affecting a smooth and viable transition for the students from the school to the job site. The need for their careful and complete pre-training and retraining cannot be overstated. That such training should, moreover, be closely related to the realities of the work-places is not disputed.

With respect to the training and retraining of technical and vocational instructors, several countries have undertaken programmes which send current teachers back to an industry or business work-place (for up to six months every three to five years in one particular case). Work by teachers in companies and firms for varying periods of time as part of their recertification requirements, while not yet commonplace, is in fact being practised increasingly in several countries. Results of initial efforts are reported to be positive in terms of more effective teaching and learning.

Institutions of higher learning have an important role to play in upgrading and retraining both teaching and counselling staff in most reporting countries. While in-service programmes offered by higher education institutions often come under criticism because they do not represent sufficient input from and influence by the realities of the work setting, certain progress in this direction is reported. Some suggest that it is as important for the professor to return occasionally to the work place as it is for the schoolteacher to do so. Sadly, little such action is reported.

Among the most pressing problems reported by several countries was the serious shortage of teachers for technical and vocational subjects. This situation has, in many cases, resulted in the schools turning to the work-places and recruiting practising journeymen and other skilled workers as part-time instructors. This effort has the advantage, of course, of bringing quite recent information from the work-place into the training classroom, laboratory or shop. The disadvantages are often found to be those associated with the part-time craftsman-teacher's lack of pedagogical skills in dealing with discipline, planning, curriculum development, etc., skills needed for effective learning by students. While these are sometimes overshadowed by increased student interest and motivation, several country reports indicate that there are too few remedies available to correct such deficiencies.

Improvement in education and training programmes for technical and vocational teachers and for guidance counsellors is reported as a high priority issue by virtually every participating nation. Recruitment of qualified persons is a concomitant priority. As with research and experimentation, increased investments in terms of fiscal and human resources for the improvement of pre-training and retraining (in-service) programmes are needed in most countries.

Because the teacher-counsellor factor is deemed to be so very crucial to the matter of improving the transition from school to work, it is fair to report that, among the several topics considered to be important, this may be most important of all. A brief review of the sections which deal with teacher and counsellor staff in each country summary (see pages 22 – 56) will reveal several significant undertakings by countries aimed at strengthening this crucial link in the education-training-transition work chain. Suffice to say here that any positive measures undertaken to improve the capabilities and capacities of technical and vocational teachers and guidance and counselling personnel will improve the transitional process.

Guidance and counselling

Apart from the question of staff involved in the counselling and guidance enterprise, discussed above, there remains the question of the substance and content of guidance and counselling programmes.

It is not enough to complain forever that guidance counsellors are not up to their task; that they are improperly prepared; that they receive too little by way of retraining; that they are mere book-keepers of student statistics; or that they have too little time to properly perform their assigned roles. It is as important, if not more so, to deal with the problems of the basic system of counselling and guidance, its proper role in the education and acculturation processes, and its form, substance and content.

Taking into account the reports of participating countries, it is fair to state that the matters of role, substance and content are at best complex and at worst misunderstood.

It is impossible, in many ways, to separate the issue of pre-training and education of guidance and counselling personnel from the issues of role definition, nature of responsibility and availability of usable data and information. For the counsellor assigned to deal with students of technical and vocational education, these issues may become even less clear. What is clear, according to the country reports and the discussions of the symposium, is the inadequacy of information regarding jobs, career environments, labour market demand and retraining opportunities for workers (to name a few). Without these kinds of data and information, guidance and counselling personnel cannot be effective in helping students make proper career and occupational choices. The aggregation of information from the country reports strongly suggests that the matter of inadequate, outdated or simply unavailable information is the most seriously limiting factor for effective guidance and counselling. Systematic approaches to resolving the information-gap problem are being undertaken in most countries, but no country is able to report, at this time, that it has mounted an information systems enterprise that is fully operational or up to this enormous task as yet.

No country would suggest that the information problem is the sole issue in this regard. Clearly, there are others, including recruitment, training, retraining in competition for services from business and industry, etc. Comprehensive and articulated measures are required to resolve these complex and limiting problems. It nevertheless appears important to focus upon the problem of inadequate information. It would seem unfair to divert attention from this central problem by simply adding to the list of other exacerbating factors in the hope somehow all will be resolved. Here again, substantially all countries agree that additional fiscal resources and better linkages with business and industry are required if the counselling and guidance picture is to be improved. This is a profound problem area whose resolution would contribute to facilitating the smooth transition from school to work.

Linkages with industry, business and commerce

Irrespective of type of government, social values, politics or present economic conditions, the reporting countries were essentially unanimous in their agreement that closer and more workable linkages with firms, companies and businesses will necessarily improve the school to work transition.

The increasing establishment and utilization of advisory committees composed of business and industrial persons has already been mentioned in this chapter. The effectiveness of the resulting improved linkages is already a matter of record in several nations.

There is also an apparent increase in programmes which provide for part of the training scheme for young workers to take place directly within the plants and firms of a country. The method used most often was that of apprenticeships. Industrial nations such as the German Democratic Republic and the Federal Republic of Germany utilize apprenticeships very extensively and with considerable success, according to their reports. Several developing nations identify apprenticeship as a key element in their planning for the improvement of young workers' technical and vocational education, and some have programmes underway. Co-operative work-experience programmes, such as those in Australia and in the United States, are increasing. Limiting factors tend to be the unavailability of sufficient work stations and inadequate on-the-job supervision of the student-worker. These types of programmes (apprenticeship, co-operative work education) are nevertheless found to be most effective in ensuring a smooth transition from school shop to workshop. The obvious benefit to the students is that they have already, before taking the first full-time job, been exposed to the reality of the work site; they know what to expect and what not to expect of real work. Many countries predict major expansions in shared education-work time experiences for their technical and vocational students. The determining factor is the extent of business and industry commitment to providing the work sites necessary for this dual education – hence, the importance of the closer industry-business-education tie.

Other aspects of technical and vocational programmes which benefit from closer ties with business, industry and commerce include opportunities for teacher retraining and up-dating; influence on the curriculum and content used in schools; provision of job-related information in more direct and up-to-date ways for guidance and counselling personnel; provision of equipment to schools by industries; and a source of part-time journeymen-teachers for the schools. These are among a few of several benefits accruing to the improved ties between education and firms, companies and businesses. Symposium participants emphasized the contributions these ties will make to improving the often difficult transition from school life to working life. The businesses, industries and commercial sectors are, after all, ultimate beneficiaries and their participation, as full partners, in the training and education of the young people who will become their skilled craftsmen, tradesmen, clerks and salespersons, seems only logical. The countries involved show an apparent agreement with such logic. That logic will, hopefully, be reflected more and more by increased co-operation by those who employ workers and those who educate and train them.

Other measures

Certain matters have been reserved for special comment, matters pertaining to measures which can improve the transition from school to work for persons who are included in special populations, namely women, the handicapped, the under-educated and migrants. It is quite obviously not enough to suggest that those measures which will operate effectively for the normal, average or advantaged student will work equally well for persons found in these groups. They are, indeed, special populations of workers. Their needs in the case of transitional support are not caused by them, nor can they be held independently accountable for their individual or group problems. Thus, in the view of the vast majority of participants in the symposium, special measures are called for.

In general, the aggregate data gained from the reports and the symposium discussions suggest that resolving the transition to work problem for these populations will mainly result from increased knowledge of an information about the special circumstances they face. The handicapped, for example, often require specialized equipment, mobility devices, barrier-free access to learning settings and special varieties of counselling and guidance. They may face serious transportation problems travelling between home and work. They will be faced with dealing with other, non-handicapped workers on the job, who often have never before associated with a handicapped person. Securing data and using them in counselling, teaching and curriculum planning has important implications for effecting improved strategies at the transitional stage.

For women, the problems are perhaps even more complex. Faced with historic patterns of bias and discrimination relative to certain classifications of jobs, they too have special requirements as they prepare to move from school to job. They will work side-by-side with men who continue to believe that women should remain in the home, raising children and accomplishing other traditional housewifely chores. Thus, support is needed, from both school and work-place, for the mental and physical adjustments women and their co-workers may have to make in order to be satisfied and productive at their work.

It is evident from the country reports and symposium discussions that these concerns are dominant in the thinking and planning of almost all nations. For some countries, women, the handicapped and migrants represent a critically important source of needed workers. Where birth rates have declined and populations are growing older, these groups will increasingly fill positions in the work-force. For some countries, it is a simple matter of economics. For most, these are matters of both economics and social strengthening. In all cases, it is apparent that these groups will receive special resources and support as they make their way from education places to work places. Several countries have undertaken measures to deal specifically with such needs. In the United States, as one example, federal policy requires the expenditure of specified amounts of federal funds (and local and state funds to match) for technical and vocational programmes for women, handicapped and disadvantaged persons. Other countries provide special centres for such persons, with particular attention given to their training and acculturation needs. Centres for women displaced from the homemaker role due to widowhood, divorce or the sheer need for income from a job to survive, are being developed in a few countries. Organizations of persons with particular concern for these special groups (advocate groups) are growing, and their influence upon the education and training programmes of their countries is beginning to be felt.

In the consensus of the participants of the symposium, there is much to be gained from increased investments of time and fiscal resources aimed at developing new measures for improving the transition for these and other special populations. Of the several topics reviewed here, perhaps none has more profound implications for both the social and economic future of a country than this.

5 Conclusions

The current situation with regard to the transition from technical and vocational schools to work is complex. This report, intended for a broad international audience, is essentially a summary of problems faced by diverse nations as they attempt to deal in different ways with a common problem. Indeed, there are many common areas of experience in dealing with the transition topic. Similarly, there are numerous specialized areas of experience. The usefulness of the material and information contained herein may be found in the mixtures of common and specialized experiences shared by the reporting countries as they and other nations continue in their efforts to solve a universal problem. It is to be hoped that new opportunities for international co-operation will be found in that mixture. Several topics might lend themselves to joint and bilateral efforts between and among nations. For example, the areas of curriculum research and design and the establishment of international information systems might become viable multinational enterprises. The present report suggests sufficient commonality of need, purpose and extant data and practice for at least these two topics to become primary candidates for further discussion and, perhaps, joint ventures.

In addition to the more specific information, methodologies and activities reported on the topic of transition from school to work, an over-riding conclusion of this report is that technical and vocational education have continued to grow in strength, popularity and availability around the world. Such expansion suggests important progress in the shift of attitude to more positive consideration for education and training programmes leading to jobs which require less than an upper secondary level qualification for entry. A 1978 Unesco report on trends and issues in technical and vocational education states:

Approaches to both the philosophy and structure of education have changed radically in recent years, and the expansion and development of technical and vocational education is at the very core of this change. Real progress has been made in terms of basic legislation and adoption of policy indicating intent and the future direction of educational development.

The present report indicates that this progress has been continuous and, in some countries, profound.

Yet, with that progress, the growth and expansion of technical and vocational programmes have come up against problems and difficulties. Not the least of these is the matter of the transition from technical and vocations education programmes to the job site – an experience which is not easy for many young workers. As the student population enrolled in such programmes has grown, so has this particular problem.

The problem of transition is perhaps one of the most complex, and at times baffling, of any faced by educators today. Even in cases where there is low unemployment, many workers, especially those entering jobs for the first time, experience difficulty in adjusting to the work. The result is often high rates of worker turnover, or the acceptance of a job that requires lower skills than those already possessed by the trainee. Worse, the result may be that the new worker delays starting the first job, suffers loss of skill through lack of practice and becomes unemployable.

While the problem is far from simple and will require a wide array of solutions, it is possible to summarize the most commonly found elements which the majority of reporting countries indicate as most confounding and pressing. That receiving most attention is the matter of inadequate or insufficient guidance and counselling service. Next is pre-training and continued training for technical and vocational instructors and guidance and counselling personnel. Third is the problem of maintaining and improving relevant curriculum which is tied to the realities of the work-place. Insufficient co-ordination of planning and policy development represents a fourth major problem. Fifth is the problem of generating sufficient research into the problems of and related to transition and the closely related items of experimentation and information. Information could well be singled out as a specific problem were it not for the fact of its impact on each of the others and in particular on those having to do with guidance and counselling, planning and curriculum improvement. A sixth problem sector deals with the issue of creating closer ties with industry and business. Finally, the special problems of women, the handicapped, migrant workers and other special populations are crucial in the great majority of reporting countries.

These seven common problems are related and interlinked in important ways. In large measure, one cannot be solved in isolation from another. Solutions to one may provide direct – or oblique – solutions to one or more others. Again, the information problem seems to be a common thread woven among – but not necessarily helping to hold together – all of these problems.

Several innovative approaches and methods currently being utilized are reported upon in the country reports. These are not isolated examples of progress, but rather suggest that positive and direct actions are being taken for at least partial resolution of the many problems each country faces. Some nations are unable to make much progress, however, because they lack the research, information and planning systems necessary for co-ordinated and purposeful action. The promotion of international co-operation in these areas could result in effective benefits to these nations in particular, and to all nations in general.

In view of the Revised Recommendation concerning Technical and Vocational

Education, the initial summary of symposium discussions and the summaries of country reports provided in this report, it is clear that acting upon the following brief conclusions could contribute to international co-operation aimed at the mutual and bilateral solving of the central problem of the transition from technical and vocational schools to work – and to solving the myriad subproblems surrounding that central issue:

1. A thorough review of the current situation in guidance and counselling services for students of technical and vocational education would serve to clarify the basic problems of context, role, function and responsibility for this sector.
2. The pre-training and upgrading of teaching and counselling personnel should be promoted with a view to increasing the work-place and technical experiences of these personnel.
3. A study of the potential for establishing an international system of technical and vocational education information exchange should be undertaken.
4. The establishment of an international mechanism for exchanging and sharing technical and vocational curriculum materials, methods for curriculum construction and updating and means for securing business-industry review of such materials should be studied in depth.
5. An international survey of the most recent developments in creating new and stronger ties between education and business and industry, stressing innovations in work-place training (apprenticeship, co-operative work programmes) should be conducted. Resulting information should be synthesized and shared broadly with Member States (Since this topic is very timely with respect to present world-wide economic conditions and the increasing dependence of industry and business upon technical and vocational education programmes for a supply of well-trained workers, it is predictable that the results of the proposed survey could lead to an international symposium which would bring business and industry leaders together with leaders of technical and vocational education system.)
6. The needs of special populations of workers (especially women, the handicapped and migrant workers) should be kept in view as further actions are taken by countries and by international organizations in their continuing effort to improve the transition from technical and vocational schools to work.

Appendixes

Appendix 1. Revised Recommendation concerning Technical and Vocational Education

The General Conference of the United National Educational, Scientific and Cultural Organization, meeting in Paris, at its eighteenth session, held from 17 October to 23 November 1974,
Recalling the constitutional responsibilities of the Organization for the promotion of education,
Recognizing that technical and vocational education have to contribute to the maintenance of peace and friendly understanding between the various nations,
Considering that education must now be seen as a lifelong process,
Recognizing that technical and vocational education is a prerequisite for sustaining the complex structure of modern civilization and economic and social development,
Recalling the principles set forth in Articles 23 and 26 of the Universal Declaration of Human Rights guaranteeing all the right to work and to education,
Considering therefore that all have a right to an education enabling full participation in contemporary society,
Taking into account the diversity of education systems throughout the world, as well as the particular and urgent needs of developing countries,
Considering that in spite of this diversity similar goals are pursued and similar questions and problems arise in all countries concerning technical and vocational education and that therefore common standards and measures are called for,
Having adopted for this purpose at its twelfth session the Recommendation concerning Technical and Vocational Education,
Recognizing however that the rapid technological and educational changes of the last decade require new, creative and efficient efforts in technical and vocational education to improve education as a whole for social, economic and cultural development,
Having decided at its seventeenth session that in view of these changes this Recommendation should be revised in order to better serve Member States.
Noting that the International Labour Conference has adopted, over the years, a number of instruments dealing with various aspects of vocational guidance and vocational training and, in particular, the Vocational Guidance Recommendation, 1949, the Vocational Training (Agriculture) Recommendation, 1956, and the Vocational Training Recommendation, 1962, and that the Conference, at its 59th session, had adopted substantive conclusions with a view to adoption, in 1975, of a new instrument or instruments on vocational guidance and vocational training,
Noting further the close collaboration between Unesco and the International Labour Organisation (ILO) in drawing up their respective instruments so that they pursue harmonious objectives, avoiding duplication and conflict, and with a view to

Appendixes

continued collaboration for effective implementation of the two instruments,
Adopts this Recommendation this nineteenth day of November 1974.
The General Conference recommends that when developing and improving technical and vocational education, Member States should apply the following provisions by taking whatever legislative or other steps may be required to give effect, within their respective territories, to the principles set forth in this Recommendation.
The General Conference recommends that Member States should bring this Recommendation to the knowledge of the authorities and bodies concerned with technical and vocational education.
The General Conference recommends that Member States should report to it, at such times and in such manner as shall be determined by it, on the action they have taken to give effect to the Recommendation.

I. Scope

1. This Recommendation applies to all forms and aspects of education which are technical and vocational in nature provided either in educational institutions or under their authority, directly by public authorities, or through other forms of organized education, public or private.
2. For the purposes of this Recommendation: 'technical and vocational education' is used as a comprehensive term referring to those aspects of the educational process involving, in addition to general education, the study of technologies and related sciences and the acquisition of practical skills, attitudes, understanding and knowledge relating to occupations in various sectors of economic and social life. Technical and vocational education is further understood to be:
   (a) an integral part of general education;
   (a) a means of preparing for an occupational field;
   (c) an aspect of continuing education.
3. Technical and vocational education, being part of the total educational process, is included in the term 'education' as defined in the Convention and Recommendation against Discrimination in Education adopted by the General Conference of the United Nations Educational, Scientific and Cultural Organization at its eleventh session and the provisions of that Convention and Recommendation are therefore applicable to it.
4. This recommendation should be understood as setting forth general principles, goals and guidelines to be applied by each individual country according to needs and resources. The application of the provisions in their particulars and the timing of the implementation will therefore depend upon the conditions existing in a given country.

II. Technical and vocational education in relation to the educational process: objectives

5. Given immense scientific and technological development, either in progress or envisaged, which characterizes the present era, technical and vocational education should be a vital aspect of the educational process and in particular should:
   (a) contribute to the achievement of society's goals of greater democratization and social, cultural and economic development, while at the same time developing the potential of individuals for active participation in the establishment and implementation of these goals;
   (b) lead to an understanding of the scientific and technological aspects of contemporary civilization in such a way that men comprehend their environment

Appendixes

and are capable of acting upon it while taking a critical view of the social, political and environmental implications of scientific and technological change.

6. Given the necessity for new relationships between education, working life, and the community as a whole, technical and vocational education should exist as part of a system of lifelong education adapted to the needs of each particular country. This system should be directed to:
   (a) abolishing barriers between levels and areas of education, between education and employment and between school and society through:
      (i) the integration of technical and vocational and general education in all educational streams above primary level;
      (ii) the creation of open and flexible educational structures;
      (iii) the taking into account of individuals' educational needs and of the evolution of occupations and jobs;
   (b) improving the quality of life by permitting the individual to expand his intellectual horizons and to acquire and to constantly improve professional skills and knowledge while allowing society to utilize the fruits of economic and technological change for the general welfare.

7. Technical and vocational education should begin with a broad basic vocational education, thus facilitating horizontal and vertical articulation within the education system and between school and employment thus contributing to the elimination of all forms of discrimination and should be designed so that it:
   (a) is an integral part of everyone's basic general education in the form of initiation to technology and to the world of work;
   (b) may be freely and positively chosen as the means by which one develops talents, interests and skills leading to an occupation in the sectors listed in paragraph 2 or to further education;
   (c) allows access to other aspects and areas of education at all levels by being grounded on a solid general education and, as a result of the integration mentioned in paragraph 6(a), containing a general education component through all stages of specialization;
   (d) allows transfers from one field to another within technical and vocational education;
   (e) is readily available to all and for all appropriate types of specialization, within and outside formal education systems, and in conjunction or in parallel with training in order to permit educational, career and job mobility at a minimum age at which the general basic education is considered to have been acquired, according to the education system in force in each country;
   (f) is available on the above terms and on a basis of equality to women as well as men;
   (g) is available to disadvantaged and handicapped persons in special forms adapted to their needs in order to integrate them more easily into society.

8. In terms of the needs and aspirations of individuals, technical and vocational education should:
   (a) permit the harmonious development of personality and character and foster the spiritual and human values, the capacity for understanding, judgement, critical thinking and self-expression;
   (b) prepare the individual to learn continuously by developing the necessary mental tools, practical skills and attitudes;

Appendixes

(c) develop capacities for decision-making and the qualities necessary for active and intelligent participation, teamwork and leadership at work and in the community as a whole.

III. Policy, planning and administration

9. Policy should be formulated and technical and vocational education administered in support of the general objectives adopted for the educational process as well as for national and, if possible, regional social and economic requirements, and an appropriate legislative and financial framework adopted. Policy should be directed to both the structural and the qualitative improvement of technical and vocational education.

10. Particular attention should be given to planning the development and expansion of technical and vocational education:
    (a) high priority should be placed on technical and vocational education in national development plans as well as in plans for educational reform;
    (b) planning should be based upon a thorough evaluation of both short-term and long-term needs taking into consideration any variation in needs which may exist within a country;
    (c) adequate provision for proper current and future allocation of financial resources should be a major element of planning;
    (d) planning should be done by a responsible body or bodies having authority on the national level. This body should have available to it data which have been collated, analysed, synthesized and interpreted by qualified staff provided with adequate research facilities.

11. Planning should be responsible to national and, if possible, regional, economic and social trends, to projected changes in demand for different classes by goods and services, and for different types of skills and knowledge in such a way that technical and vocational education may easily adapt to the evolving situation be it rural or urban. This planning should also be co-ordinated with current and projected training action and the evolution of employment.

12. While the education authorities should have primary responsibility, the following groups and authorities should be actively associated in policy formulation, and in the planning process. Structures, on both national and local levels, taking the form of public agencies or consultative or advisory bodies, should be created to permit this:
    (a) public authorities responsible for planning economic and social policy, labour and employment, and for the various occupational sectors (industry, agriculture, commerce);
    (b) representatives of non-governmental organizations within each occupation sector from among employers and workers;
    (c) any authority or body, such as a training body or extension services, responsible for out-of-school education and training;
    (d) representatives of those responsible – both in public education and in State recognized private education – for executing educational policy including teachers, examining bodies and administrators;
    (e) parent, former pupil, student and youth organizations;
    (f) representatives from the community at large.

13. Policies for the structural improvement of technical and vocational education should be established within the framework of broad policies designed to implement the principles of lifelong education through the creation of open, flexible and comple-

mentary structures for education, training and educational and vocational guidance, regardless of whether these activities take place within the system of formal education or outside it. In this respect consideration should be given to the following:
- (a) multipurpose secondary education offering diversified curricula including work-study programmes;
- (b) open tertiary institutions recruiting from a variety of sources and offering programmes ranging from short specialized ones to longer full-time programmes of integrated studies and professional specialization;
- (c) establishing a system of equivalencies whereby credit is given for completion of any approved programme and recognition is granted educational and professional qualifications achieved through various means.

14. Policy should be directed to ensuring high quality in such a way as to exclude the possibility of any judgement which discriminates between the different educational streams, whatever their ultimate goal. In this respect special efforts should be made to ensure that technical and vocational education in rural areas meets the same standards as that offered in urban ones.

15. In order to ensure quality, responsible national authorities should establish certain criteria and standards, subject to periodic review and evaluation, applying in all aspects of technical and vocational education, including to the extent possible non-formal education for:
- (a) all forms of recognition of achievement and consequent qualification;
- (b) staff qualifications;
- (c) ratios of teaching and training staff to learners;
- (d) the quality of curricula and teaching materials;
- (e) safety precautions for all learning environments;
- (f) physical facilities, building, workshop layouts, quality and type of equipment.

16. Policies should be established fostering research related to technical and vocational education, with particular emphasis on its potential within lifelong education, and directed to its improvement. This research should be carried out by competent staff on national and institutional levels as well as through individual initiative. To this end:
- (a) special emphasis should be placed on curriculum development, research concerning teaching and learning methods and materials, and where the need exists, on technologies and techniques applied to development problems;
- (b) financial resources and physical facilities should be made available through institutions of higher education, specialized research institutions and professional organizations for applying the results of this research on an experimental basis in representatively selected institutions for technical and vocational education;
- (c) channels should be created for the widespread dissemination and rapid application of the positive results of research and experimentation;
- (d) the effectiveness of technical and vocational education should be evaluated using, among other data, relevant statistics including those concerning part-time enrolments and drop-out rates which are in some cases neglected;
- (e) particular attention should be given to all research efforts to humanize working conditions.

17. Provision should be made within administrative structures for evaluation, supervisory and accreditation services, staffed by technical and vocational education specialists, to ensure the rapid application of new research findings and to maintain standards:
- (a) evaluation services as a whole should ensure the quality and smooth operation of

Appendixes

        technical and vocational education by continuous review and action directed to constant improvement of staff, facilities and programmes;
- (b) supervisory services for the staff should encourage improvement in the quality of teaching by providing guidance and advice and recommending continuing education;
- (c) all programmes of technical and vocational education, in particular, those offered by private bodies, should be subject to approval by the public authorities through some means of accreditation or form of public inspection.

18. Particular attention should be given to the material resources required for technical and vocational education. Priorities should be carefully established with due regard for immediate needs and the probable directions of future expansion and adequate cost controls introduced:
    - (a) institutional planning should be directed to ensuring maximum efficiency and flexibility in use;
    - (b) the planning, construction and equipping of facilities should be carried out in collaboration with specialist teachers and educational architects and with due regard for their purpose, prevailing local factors and relevant research;
    - (c) adequate funds should be allocated for recurrent expenditure for supplies and maintenance and repair of equipment.

IV. Technical and vocational aspects of general education

19. An initiation to technology and to the world of work should be an essential component of general education without which this education is incomplete. An understanding of the technological facet of modern culture in both its positive and negative attributes, and an appreciation of work requiring practical skills should thereby be acquired. This initiation should further be a major concern in educational reform and change with a view to greater democratization of education. It should be a required element in the curriculum, beginning in primary education and continuing through the early years of secondary education.
20. Opportunities for general technical and vocational initiation should continue to be available to those who wish to avail themselves of it within the educational system and outside it in places of work or community centres.
21. The technical and vocational initiation in the general education of youth should fulfil the educational requirements of all ranges of interest and ability. It should mainly perform three functions:
    - (a) to enlarge educational horizons by serving as an introduction to the world of work and the world of technology and its products through the exploration of materials, tools, techniques and the process of production, distribution and management as a whole, and to broaden the learning process through practical experience;
    - (b) to orient those with the interest and ability toward technical and vocational education as preparation for an occupational field or toward training outside the formal education system;
    - (c) to promote in those who will leave formal education at whatever level but with no specific occupational aims or skills, attitudes of mind and ways of thought likely to enhance their aptitudes and potential, to facilitate the choice of an occupation and access to a first job, and to permit them to continue their vocational training and personal education.
22. Required general technical and vocational studies in the schools having great

importance for the orientation and education of youth programmes, should include a proper balance between theoretical and practical work. A properly structured programme of such studies should be drawn up by the competent authorities in collaboration with the professional community and with those responsible for technical and vocational education. These programmes should:
   (a) be based upon a problem-solving and experimental approach and involve experience in planning methods and decision-making;
   (b) introduce the learner to a broad spectrum of technological fields and at the same time to productive work situations;
   (c) develop a certain command of valuable practical skills such as tool use, repair and maintenance and safety procedures, whether applicable to future education, training and employment or to leisure time, and a respect for their value;
   (d) develop an appreciation of good design and craftsmanship and the ability to select goods on the basis of their quality;
   (e) develop the ability to communicate including the use of graphical means;
   (f) develop the ability to measure and calculate accurately;
   (g) be closely related to the local environment without, however, being limited to it.
23. The technical and vocational initiation in programmes of general educational enrichment for older youth and adults should be directed to enabling those engaged in working life to:
   (a) understand the general implications of technological change, its impact on their professional and private lives, and how man may shape this change;
   (b) to use practical skills for improving the home and community environment and thus the quality of life and, in appropriate conditions, for productive leisure-time activities.

V. Technical and vocational education as preparation for an occupational field

24. Given disparities that may exist between formal education, whether secondary or tertiary, and the employment and career opportunities available, the highest priority should be given to technical and vocational education which prepares young people to exercise occupations in the sectors covered by this recommendation. Consequently the structure and content of traditional education, whether general or technical and vocational, should be adapted accordingly through:
   (a) the diversification of secondary education in the later stages so that it may be pursued in conjunction with employment or training, or may lead to employment or to higher eduction, thereby offering to all youth educational options corresponding to their needs;
   (b) the introduction of new programmes into tertiary education more relevant to the career needs of young adults;
   (c) the development of educational structures and programmes on all levels centred on organized and flexible interchange between educational institutions including training institutions and those responsible for employment in the various occupational sectors.
25. Technical and vocational education as preparation for an occupational field should provide the foundation for productive and satisfying careers and should:
   (a) lead to the acquisition of broad knowledge and basic skills applicable to a number of occupations within a given field so that the individual is not limited by his education in his freedom of occupational choice, and later transfer from one field

Appendixes

      to another in the course of working life is facilitated;
- (b) at the same time offer a thorough and specialized preparation for initial employment and effective training within employment;
- (c) provide the background in terms of skills, knowledge and attitudes, for continuing education at any point in the individual's working life.

26. Premature and narrow specialization should be avoided:
    - (a) in principle 15 should be considered the lower age limit for beginning specialization;
    - (b) a period of common studies concerning basic knowledge and skills should be required for each broad occupational sector before a special branch is chosen.
27. Because it is desirable that women seek wider participation in all kinds of occupations outside family and domestic activities, they should have the same educational opportunities available to them as men in order to prepare for an occupation and should be encouraged to take advantage of these through appropriate legislative measures and widespread distribution of information concerning these opportunities.
28. Special provision should be made for out-of-school and unemployed youth and children of migrant workers with the minimum or less of primary education, as well as for those not entering education or training programmes after completion of compulsory schooling, in order that they may acquire employable skills.
29. Given the necessity of integrating the physically and mentally disadvantaged into society and its occupations, the same educational opportunities should be available to them as to the non-handicapped in order that they may achieve qualification for an occupation; special measures or special institutions may be required.

Organization

30. Technical and vocational education as preparation for an occupational field should be organized on a national or, if possible, regional basis, so as to respond positively to over-all social, economic and educational requirements and to the needs of different groups of the population without discrimination.
31. Several organizational patterns of technical and vocational education, including both full-time and part-time options should exist within each country. The following patterns of organization for example should be considered:
    - (a) full-time including practical training as well as general education, provided in an educational establishment, either comprehensive or specialized;
    - (b) part-time programmes such as the following in which general education and theoretical and broad practical aspects of the occupational field are given in an educational establishment while specialized practical training is acquired during work in the chosen occupation:
        - (i) the day-release system providing for young workers and apprentices to attend an educational establishment at least one day a week and preferably two;
        - (ii) the sandwich system under which periods in an educational institution alternate with training periods in a factory, farm, business establishment or other undertaking;
        - (iii) the block-release system whereby young workers are released to attend courses for one or two short periods of at least ten to fifteen weeks in total length per year which may be especially adapted to conditions in areas of low population density by provision of boarding facilities.
32. The responsible authorities should encourage part-time education, therefore:
    - (a) these programmes should be available directly after completion of minimum

compulsory or required schooling, and should continue to be available to the highest level of formal education;
(b) the educational qualifications acquired by this means should be equivalent to those acquired by full-time education;
(c) where employers are responsible for the practical training aspect for part-time students, this training should be as broad as possible serving the educational and training needs of the individual, and should meet national standards.

33. In view of the increasing requirement for highly qualified middle-level manpower in all fields, and the increasing numbers completing secondary education or its equivalent, the development of programmes of technical and vocational education corresponding to further qualifying tertiary education should be given high priority. The following patterns of organization should be considered:
   (a) a period of from one to two years of guided work experience followed by a part-time or briefer full-time programme of specialization;
   (b) part-time programmes;
   (c) full-time programmes as an extension of programmes given in specialized secondary institutions or given in tertiary institutions.

34. The high cost of equipment for the practical component of technical and vocational education requires that this be organized so that benefits received are in proportion to the cost. Consideration should be given to the following as a means of achieving this:
   (a) centralized workshops, or mobile units, could be used to serve several educational institutions;
   (b) workshops attached to educational institutions could be designed so that they are suitable for use by the community at large particularly for continuing education programmes;
   (c) although workshops and laboratories in advanced secondary or tertiary institutions should be designed primarily for pedagogical purposes, they might also be equipped and staffed so that equipment for use in technical and vocational studies in general education may be produced.

35. Enterprises should be closely associated in the practical training of those preparing for occupations in their particular sector, and should be encouraged to take responsibility, in co-operation with educational institutions, for the organization of this training.

Programme content

36. All programmes of technical and vocational education as preparation for an occupational field should:
   (a) aim at providing scientific knowledge, technical versatility and the broad skills and knowledge required for rapid adaptation to new ideas and procedures and for steady career development;
   (b) be based on an analysis of broad occupational requirements worked out for the long term between education authorities including organizations representing educational research and administration and employment authorities and occupational organizations concerned;
   (c) include a proper balance between general subjects, science and technology, and studies of both the theoretical and practical aspects of the occupational field, with the practical component in all cases related to the theoretical one;
   (d) stress developing a sense of professional values and responsibilities from the standpoint of human needs.

37. In particular programmes should:
    (a) whenever possible be interdisciplinary in character as many occupations now require knowledge and training in two or more traditional areas of study;
    (b) be based on curricula designed around core knowledge and skills;
    (c) include studies of the social and economic aspects of the occupational field as a whole;
    (d) include the study of at least one foreign language of international use which, while conducive to a higher cultural level, will give special emphasis to the requirements of communication and the acquisition of a scientific and technical vocabulary;
    (e) include an introduction to organizational and planning skills;
    (f) emphasize instruction in safety procedures relative to the materials and equipment used in a given occupational field and the importance of safe working conditions and the health aspects relative to the occupation as a whole.
38. While based on the above general principles and components, and thus pursuing in all cases broader educational aims, programmes in their practical aspect should be designed taking into account special occupational requirements with regard to the particular executive, organizational, analytical and practical skills required.
39. Technical and vocational education programmes leading to university qualification, while encouraging research and offering high-level specialization, should be developed with particular attention to:
    (a) the inclusion of components directed to developing attitudes whereby those with broad responsibilities in technological fields constantly relate their professional tasks to larger human goals;
    (b) relating more closely higher technical and vocational education for the industrial and agricultural sectors to the requirements of these sectors. In this regard consideration should be given to creating within tertiary institutions, centres for the testing and certification of industrial and agricultural products, supervised by the public authorities and serving both educational and research purposes.
40. Programmes of technical and vocational education as preparation for occupations within the agricultural sector should be designed in accordance with the over-all social and economic requirements of rural development. Therefore:
    (a) both general aspects and the technical and vocational aspects, while adapted in terms of both organization and content to the special requirements of agricultural occupations, should be of the same quality as those for other occupational areas;
    (b) programmes should be directed to the development and application of technologies especially suited to rural development through close co-ordination between education and extension services and between these and research services and institutions;
    (c) programmes should be directed to preparing qualified people for all types of occupations and ranges of technical competence necessary for rural development;
    (d) programmes should be broadly conceived, including in addition to the special occupational area, an introduction to the commercial aspects of agriculture and the functioning of rural economic institutions.
41. Where lack of resources limits the expansion of technical and vocational education, emphasis in the initial stages should be placed on developing programmes for occupations in areas of critical manpower shortage, and in areas of immediate development potential.
42. Programmes preparing for occupations in small industry, individual farming or the artisan trades, whether urban or rural, and particularly for self-employment, should

include commercial studies enabling those engaged in such occupations to take responsibility not only for production, but also for marketing, competent management and the rational organization of the whole enterprise.
43. Programmes leading to occupations in the business and commercial sector should include:
    (a) a thorough grounding in the methods and skills developed as a result of the application of technology to business and office management and particularly to the acquisition and processing of information;
    (b) training in the organizational and management skills required for the smooth operation of enterprises in all economic sectors;
    (c) an introduction to marketing and distribution procedures.
44. Special attention should be given to developing programmes for preparing personnel at all levels for the social services sector (e.g. community and family work, nursing and paramedical occupations, nutrition and food technology, home economics and environmental improvement). Those programmes should:
    (a) emphasize the relation of the special occupational field to raising standards of living in terms of food, clothing, housing, medical services, the quality of family life or that of the environment as the case may be;
    (b) be well adapted to the special requirements of local conditions in particular those of climate and geography, materials available and community organization and social patterns.

VI. Technical and vocational education as continuing education

45. The development and expansion of technical and vocational education as continuing education, both within and outside the formal education system, and within the framework of lifelong education, should be a priority objective of all educational strategies and broad provision should be made for allowing everyone, whatever the educational qualifications achieved prior to employment, to continue both their professional and general education.
46. In addition to permitting adults to make up deficiencies in general education or professional qualifications, which has often been the only objective of continuing education, it should now:
    (a) offer possibilities of personal development and professional advancement;
    (b) permit the updating and refreshing of knowledge and practical abilities and skills in the occupational field;
    (c) enable the individual to adapt to technological changes in his occupation or to enter another occupation if these changes render his particular job obsolete;
    (d) be available throughout working life without restriction of age, sex, prior education and training or position;
    (e) be broad in scope, including general education elements, and not simply specialized training for one particular job.
47. The appropriate authorities should be encouraged to provide the basic conditions for technical and vocational education as continuing education, including consideration of measures providing for paid educational leave or other forms of financial aid.
48. The technical and vocational aspect of continuing education should actively be encouraged through such means as:
    (a) widespread dissemination of information concerning the programmes available, and how one may take advantage of existing opportunities, including full use of mass media to this end;

Appendixes

    (b) recognition of successful completion of programmes in terms of remuneration and professional advancement.
49. Those responsible for organizing programmes of continuing technical and vocational education recognized by the public authorities should consider the following forms:
    (a) courses given during working hours at the place of work;
    (b) fuller part-time courses especially designed for continuing education given in secondary and tertiary institutions, already staffed and equipped for technical and vocational education;
    (c) evening and week-end courses given in the above types of institutions or in community centres;
    (d) correspondence courses;
    (e) courses given on educational television;
    (f) periodic seminars;
    (g) inter-enterprise programmes;
    (h) informal discussion groups created and organized on the initiative of students.
50. The following forms of organization of leave should be considered:
    (a) day release;
    (b) block release of varying lengths;
    (c) release for one or more hours during the working day.
51. Programmes of technical and vocational education as continuing education should:
    (a) be designed and taught on the basis of the special requirements of adults, and use teaching methods which take into account the expertise which they have already acquired;
    (b) contain a built-in mechanism for rapid adjustment to the needs of particular individuals or groups and to technological change.
52. Special provision should be made for groups with particular requirements:
    (a) in the case of women, because of the necessity of periods of absence from the labour force imposed by maternity and family responsibilities, in order to enable them to update their knowledge and to improve their professional skills for re-entry into employment;
    (b) to enable older workers to adapt to new occupations;
    (c) to provide foreign workers and handicapped workers with specific facilities for pre-training to enable them to adapt to a training programme or to working life;
    (d) the resources of continuing education should be used to offer unskilled and semi-skilled workers the opportunity to improve their qualifications.
53. Particular attention should be paid to the development of continuing education programmes suitable in rural areas in terms of content, physical location and time of year offered.

VII. Guidance

54. Guidance should be viewed as a continuous process and a vital element in education, directed to aiding all to make positive educational and occupational choices. It should ensure that the individual be provided with the necessary prerequisites:
    (a) to become aware of his interests and abilities and able to set himself precise objectives;
    (b) to pursue a course of education, whether preparatory or continuing, commensurate with these;

Appendixes

  (c) to make decisions concerning his occupation, both in the initial and later stages, which lead to a satisfying career;
  (d) to facilitate transitions between education and employment at whatever level or stage.
55. Guidance services on the national, local and institutional levels should ensure that the paths are kept open between education and initial training and employment, and employment and continuing education and training through:
  (a) close liaison and co-ordination with training, counselling, employment and placement services;
  (b) ensuring that all necessary information concerning employment and career opportunities is available and actively disseminated;
  (c) ensuring that those in employment have access to information concerning opportunities in continuing education and training.
56. While emphasizing the needs of the individual, guidance for young people should be accompanied by information which gives them a realistic view of the opportunities available in a given occupational cluster, including information regarding probable developments in the market and in employment structures, and what may be expected in terms of remuneration, career advancement and possibilities for occupational change.
57. Particular attention should be given to guidance for girls and women:
  (a) this guidance should cover the same broad range of education, training and employment opportunities as for boys and men;
  (b) it should systematically encourage girls and women to take advantage of the opportunities available to them.
58. Guidance given in the technical and vocational aspects of general education during the observation or orientation cycle of secondary schooling should:
  (a) cover a broad range of occupations with supplementary visits to work places and acquaint the student with the eventual necessity of choosing an occupation and the importance of this choice being as rational as possible;
  (b) aid students in making a positive choice concerning educational streams or options for those wishing to pursue technical and vocational education as preparation for an occupational field or training programmes outside the education system, and aid those not continuing their formal education or entering training to find employment, while encouraging them to continue their education at a later date.
59. Guidance in technical and vocational education as preparation for an occupational field should:
  (a) inform the student of the various possibilities open in the particular field of interest, the educational background required and the possibilities for later continuing education available;
  (b) encourage the student to choose an educational programme which will limit his later employment options as little as possible;
  (c) follow the progress of the student during the educational programmes;
  (d) supplement the later stages of the programmes by short periods of work experience and study of real work situations.
60. Guidance in technical and vocational education as continuing education should:
  (a) help the employed adult choose the programme of continuing education most suited to his needs:

Appendixes

    (b) enable him to place himself in relation to the various levels of study and afford him the means of making effective choices.
61. Guidance should be given on the basis of:
    (a) knowledge of the individual which takes account of the social and family factors influencing his attitudes and expectations;
    (b) information obtained from objective evaluation of the results of testing including aptitude tests;
    (c) knowledge of his educational achievements and/or achievements in employment;
    (d) knowledge of employment and career opportunities as well as job satisfaction in the occupational sector in which he is interested or engaged and of demands made;
    (e) medical records indicating whether the student is physically able to pursue a given occupation.
62. The effectiveness of guidance services should continually be assessed and statistics kept on both the national and institutional levels through:
    (a) the keeping of cumulative records concerning the education of the student as well as follow-up records concerning his employment;
    (b) a built-in system of evaluation of both quality of staff performance and the methods used in order to effect change or improvement where needed.

VIII. The teaching and learning processes: methods and materials

63. In all aspects of technical and vocational education, the methodology of learning should assume equal importance in the teaching and learning process with the subject-matter itself. All aspects of technical and vocational education should be oriented to the needs of the learner and directed to motivating him, and methods and materials developed accordingly.
64. Theory and practice should form an integrated whole: what is learned in the laboratory, workshop or in enterprises should be directly related to the mathematical and scientific foundations of the particular operation or process, and conversely, technical theory, as well as the mathematics and science sustaining it, should be illustrated through their practical applications.
65. Full use should be made of the resources provided by educational technology, with special emphasis on the methods and materials of self-education, in particular audio-visual aids, including multi-media systems, programmed instruction and the use of mass media.
66. The methods and materials used in technical and vocational education should be carefully adapted to the group to be taught. In this respect:
    (a) where the language of instruction differs from the native language, teaching materials should make maximum use of numerical and graphical representation, written material being kept to a minimum;
    (b) where materials developed in one country are adapted for use in another, this adaptation should be carefully made with due regard to local factors.
67. Machines and equipment used in workshops in educational institutions should be geared to the level and training of the users. This equipment should be simple and designed especially for pedagogical purposes without however being obsolete or teaching obsolete procedures. Training using complex equipment may be given more appropriately and efficiently on the job.

Evaluation

68. Evaluation should be an integral part of the teaching and learning process in technical and vocational education, and its major function should be the development of the particular individual in accordance with his interests and capacities.
69. Although standards of performance should be upheld, evaluation of the student's work should be made on a total basis considering among others his class participation, his interest and attitude, his relative progress, allowance being made for his aptitudes, and examinations and other tests.
70. Students should participate in the evaluation of their own progress and the evaluation of student work should have a system of feedback built into it so that learning problems and their causes may be identified and steps taken to correct them.
71. Continuous evaluation of the teaching process should be made by both teachers and their supervisors, with the participation of students as well, in order to determine the effectiveness of the methods and materials used, and to devise alternatives should the need arise. Continuous evaluation of the teaching-learning process should be undertaken with the participation of representatives from the occupational fields concerned.

IX. Staff

72. To enhance the achievement of the objectives of technical and vocational education, a priority should be given to the recruitment and preparation of adequate numbers of well-qualified and competent teachers, administrators, and guidance staff and to the provision of the necessary training and other facilities to enable them to function effectively in their profession.
73. The emoluments and conditions of service which are offered should compare favourably with those enjoyed by persons with similar qualification and experience in other occupational sectors. In particular, promotions, salaries and pension scales for technical and vocational education staff should take into account any relevant experience acquired in employment outside the educational sector.

Teaching staff

74. All teachers in technical and vocational education, including those who teach only practice, should be considered an integral part of the teaching profession and as such should be recognized as having the same status as their colleagues in other fields. In this regard:
    (a) the Recommendation concerning the Status of Teachers adopted by the Special Inter-governmental Conference on the Status of Teachers on 5 October 1966 is applicable to them especially as regards the provisions concerning preparation for a profession and continuing education; employment and career; the rights and responsibilities of teachers; conditions for effective teaching and learning; teachers' salaries; social security;
    (b) arbitrary distinctions between teachers employed by various types of educational institutions, e.g. specialized technical and vocational institutions and general education institutions should be eliminated.
75. Teachers involved in any aspect of technical and vocational education, whether on a full-time or part-time basis, should possess the personal, ethical, professional and teaching qualities essential for the accomplishment of their work.
76. Teachers of technical and vocational aspects in general education should:
    (a) be familiar with a broad range of specialities;

Appendixes

  (b) develop the ability to relate these to each other as well as to the larger social, economic and historical and cultural context;
  (c) where this aspect of technical and vocational education serves primarily an occupation or educational orientation function, be able to give guidance.
77. Considering technical and vocational education as preparation for an occupational field, teachers in this area should have special qualifications depending on the occupation for which they are preparing students:
  (a) if the occupational field requires primarily practical skills the teacher should himself have long employment experience in the exercise of these skills;
  (b) if students are to be prepared for technician or middle management positions, teachers should have a thorough knowledge, preferably acquired through appropriate practical experience, of the special requirements of this type of position;
  (c) if the occupational field requires research and theoretical analysis, e.g. an engineering field, the teacher should have a university education and be actively engaged in research himself.
79. Skilled professionals employed in appropriate sectors outside education should be invited to teach, at suitable points in technical and vocational education, certain programmes in schools, universities or other educational institutions in order to link the world of work more closely to the classroom.
80. Teachers of general subjects in institutions which offer technical and vocational education, in addition to the usual qualification, both professional and in their teaching field, should receive a special initiation concerning the objectives and requirements of technical and vocational education.
81. Preparation for technical and vocational teaching should be given as a tertiary programme, thereby requiring completion of secondary education or its equivalent for entrance. All types of programme should be designed with the following objectives in mind:
  (a) to maintain standards of education and professional preparation in vigour for the teaching profession as a whole and to contribute to the raising of these over-all standards;
  (b) to develop in the future teacher the ability to teach both theoretical and the practical aspects of his field;
  (c) to ensure that the teacher will be qualified, with minimum further training, to teach other groups than those for which he was prepared initially.
82. Varied and flexible programmes, full time and part time, adapted to the special requirements of a wide variety of recruitment sources as well as to those of the field to be taught and the group or groups to be taught should be available.
83. In those cases where it is difficult for intending technical and vocational teachers to acquire employment experience, consideration should be given to creating units, attached to teacher-training institutions, for the production of equipment and teaching materials for the schools in which intending teaching staff would be required to work for varying lengths of time.
84. The professional preparation of all technical and vocational teachers should include the following elements:
  (a) educational theory both in general and as especially applying to technical and vocational education;
  (b) educational psychology and sociology as it especially applies to the group or groups for which the future teacher will be responsible;

Appendixes

    (c) special teaching methods appropriate to the field of technical and vocational education for which the future teacher is preparing and the groups to be taught, in methods of evaluation of student work, and in classroom management;
    (d) training in the choice and use of the whole range of modern teaching techniques and aids presupposing the use of up-to-date methods and materials in the programme of professional preparation itself;
    (e) training in how to create and produce appropriate teaching materials, of special importance in those cases where technical and vocational teaching materials are in short supply;
    (f) a period of supervised practice teaching experience before appointment to a teaching post;
    (g) an introduction to educational and occupational guidance methods as well as to educational administration;
    (h) a thorough grounding in safety and emphasis on the ability to teach safe working practice and habitually to set a good working example.
85. Staff responsible for the preparation of technical and vocational teachers should have obtained the highest qualifications possible in their field:
    (a) teacher-educators responsible for special technical and vocational fields should have qualifications in their field equivalent to those of special subjects staff in other institutions and programmes of higher education, including advanced degrees and employment experience in a related occupational field;
    (b) teacher-educators responsible for the pedagogical aspect of teacher preparation should themselves be experienced teachers in technical and vocational education and should possess the highest qualifications in a specialized field of education.
86. Staff responsible for the preparation of technical and vocational teachers should be actively engaged in research in their field and provision should be made for this in terms of a reasonable teaching load and access to appropriate facilities.
87. Teaching staff should be encouraged to continue their education, whatever the field in which they specialize, and should have the necessary means to do so. This continuing education which should be made available in a wide range of facilities, should include:
    (a) periodic review and updating of knowledge and skills in the special field;
    (b) periodic updating of professional skills and knowledge;
    (c) periodic work in the occupational sector relating to the special field.
88. Account should be taken of a teacher's achievements in continuing education when the responsible authorities consider questions of promotion, seniority and status concerning him.

Administrative and guidance staff

89. Adminstrative responsibilities for technical and vocational education programmes should be entrusted to persons with the following qualifications:
    (a) teaching experience in a field of technical and vocational education;
    (b) proficiency acquired through study and employment experience in one of the fields taught in the programme;
    (c) a broad vision of technical and vocational education as a whole and of the interrelation of the various aspects;
    (d) a knowledge of administrative techniques.
90. The heads of establishments in technical and vocational education should receive adequate administrative assistance so that they can devote most of their time to the highly important educational and scientific aspects of their work. Technical and

Appendixes

vocational education establishments should have sufficient staff to provide the following services:
(a) advice and guidance for candidates and students;
(b) the preparation, supervision and co-ordination of all practical work and experiments;
(c) the maintenance of instruments, apparatus and tools in workshops and laboratories.
91. Administrators should keep up to date with new administrative techniques and trends through programmes of continuing education. Prospective administrators should receive special training in methods and problems involved in the task. This preparation should include:
(a) management methods appropriate to educational administration;
(b) methods of allocation of available resources given the objectives of the various programmes for which they will be responsible;
(c) planning methods.
92. Guidance staff should receive special preparation for their tasks whether they are specialists or are teachers serving also as guidance staff. This preparation should stress psychology, pedagogy, sociology and economics. Guidance staff should be equipped to make objective assessments of aptitude, interest and motivation and to have at hand up-to-date information concerning career and education opportunities. During this preparation they should acquire a direct knowledge of the economy and the world of work through systematically organized visits to enterprises and periods of time spent in enterprises. Guidance staff should be required and provided with facilities – including the opportunity for practical experience – to keep up with new methods of guidance and information as to new or changed educational training and employment opportunities.

X. International co-operation

93. Member States should give priority to international co-operation in the field of technical and vocational education.
(a) This co-operation, whether in the framework of bilateral or multilateral agreements, or through international organizations, should be directed to improving the quality of technical and vocational education and developing and expanding it where necessary.
(a) Every effort should be made to co-ordinate within any given country the international assistance activities in the field of technical and vocational education.
94. Member States should take special measures to provide foreigners (in particular migrants and refugees) and their children living within their territory with technical and vocational education. Such measures should take into account the special needs of such persons in the host country as well as in view of their possible return to their country.
95. Provision should be made at national, regional and international levels for the regular exchange of information, documentation, and materials of international interest obtained from research and development efforts on all levels concerning technical and vocational education, in particular:
(a) publications concerning, among others, comparative education, psychological and pedagogical problems affecting general and technical and vocational education, and current trends;

(b) information and documentation concerning curriculum development, methods and materials, study opportunities abroad, employment opportunities including manpower requirements, working conditions and social benefits;
(c) teaching materials and equipment;
(d) mass media programmes of an informational or pedagogical character.

96. Regional co-operation among countries having a common cultural heritage and facing common problems in the development or extension of technical and vocational education should be highly encouraged through:
    (a) periodic meetings on the ministerial level and the establishment of a standing committee or organization to review policies formulated and actions taken;
    (b) the creation of joint facilities for higher level research, the development of prototype materials and equipment, and the preparation of staff for the training of teachers where the costs of such facilities are too high to be sustained by any one country in a given region.

97. The development of both written and audio-visual teaching and learning materials which are suitable for international or regional use should be considered a priority area in international co-operation. These materials should contribute to the progressive establishment of common standards for professional qualifications acquired through technical and vocational education.

98. Member States should encourage the creation of a climate of opinion favourable to international co-operation in the field of technical and vocational education through:
    (a) teacher and student fellowships and exchanges;
    (b) establishment of sustained contacts between similar institutions in different countries;
    (c) provision of employment experience abroad, particularly when opportunities at home are limited.

99. To facilitate international co-operation, Member States should apply within technical and vocational education internationally recommended standards and norms relating in particular to:
    (a) systems of measure;
    (b) scientific and technical symbols;
    (c) occupational qualifications;
    (d) information processing;
    (e) equivalencies of qualifications acquired through technical and vocational education implying standardization of curricula and testing, including aptitude tests, for some technical fields;
    (f) safety and security through testing of materials and products.

100. Internationally recommended standards and norms concerning technical and vocational education should be continuously evaluated through sustained research concerning the effectiveness of their application in the various countries especially in order to facilitate the establishment of equivalence of qualifications and free movement of individuals between the different national systems of education.

Appendix 2. Guidelines for preparing country reports to be presented to the symposium on problems of transition from technical and vocational schools to work

Introduction
This symposium is organized to review problems of transition from technical and vocational schools to work. The purpose of the country reports is to inform participants on developments in technical and vocational education with a view to facilitating the exchange of information and discussion on this subject.

The guidelines below are designed to facilitate a comparison and analysis of the country reports with each other. They should be followed as closely as possible by the authors.

1. *Structures*
   Briefly describe and, wherever possible, illustrate graphically:
   1.1 The overall structure of your country's education system (see example, page 3) and the place of technical and vocational education (including teacher training) within it. Indicate the linkage between levels of schooling and between school and work and the relationship between in-school and out-of-school programmes.
   1.2 Organizational structures (see example, page 4), showing relationships and linkage among them, for:
      1.2.1 overall policy-making and planning for technical and vocational education;
      1.2.2 research and curriculum development; collection and dissemination of information;
      1.2.3 co-ordinating in-school and out-of-school programmes and co-ordinating technical and vocational education with manpower planning and employment in general;
   1.3 The structure of vocational and educational guidance, whether within or outside the educational system.

2. *Organization*
   Describe the organizational measures your country has taken to facilitate the transition from technical and vocational school to work, including:
   2.1 manpower surveys and their impact on technical and vocational education;
   2.2 co-ordinating mechanisms between technical and vocational institutions and industry;
   2.3 work-study arrangements;
   2.4 physical placement of schools in areas with employment possibilities;
   2.5 follow-up system after graduation.

3. *Contents and methods*
   3.1 Indicate whether vocational guidance is included in the training programme and, if so, how effective it is.
   3.2 Describe what changes have been made in the programme in recent years to make the curriculum more relevant to employment. Describe research activities which are oriented toward making graduates of vocational and technical schools more employable.

4. *Teaching staff*
   4.1 Indicate whether there are separate guidance teachers and, if so, how they are trained.
   4.2 Indicate whether or not teachers from industry are engaged on a part-time basis.
   4.3 Describe the extent of involvement of technical teachers in co-ordination and co-operation between schools and employers.

5. *Conclusions*
   Sum up the major achievements made in your country on the problems of transition from technical and vocational schools to work, indicating drawbacks and difficulties encountered and actions planned to offset them.

Appendix 3. International Symposium on Problems of Transition from Technical and Vocational Schools to Work (Berlin, German Democratic Republic), 14–18 April 1980)

Summary of discussions

Introduction

The participants presented country reports which gave an overall view of the existing situation of technical and vocational education and training in their respective countries and the special problems of transition to work. A detailed discussion followed on the basis of the paper prepared by the Unesco Secretariat, which comprised the following three parts: 'Nature and Scope of the Problem'; 'Current Efforts and Innovative Approaches'; 'Possible Measures for Improving the Transition Between Technical and Vocational Schools and Work'.

The participants agreed to the working procedures proposed by the chairman, i.e. to have discussions on each part of the paper and to follow the questions listed at the end of each part as a further guide for discussion. It was suggested that an important outcome of the discussion might be to enrich and complete the ideas expressed in the discussion paper, on the basis of the experience of the participants.

Nature and scope of the problem

It was stated that the problems of transition were complex and varied from one country to another depending upon the social and economic conditions as well as educational and training systems. These problems are influenced by the education and training process as a whole. Hence it is necessary to consider technical and vocational education as an integrated system, comprising all components and programmes which aim at the development, in appropriate environments, of cognitive and practical skills. The process should link different levels and types of education, training and apprenticeship. It should also articulate the concept of lifelong learning related to career growth of individuals. It was stated that the Unesco Revised Recommendation concerning Technical and Vocational Education and the corresponding International Labour Organisation (ILO) instruments could be used as a basis for the development of an integrated system of technical and vocational education and training.

Several participants emphasized that the problems of transition from technical and vocational schools to work concern education and training as well as employment. The importance of well-functioning co-ordination mechanisms at the national, local and institutional levels was stressed. One participant suggested a graphic scheme for portraying the major stages in the transition from school to work.

It was noted that technical and vocational education should take into account population/demographic conditions and changes and the socio-economic development plans. Reference is made to the special problems of developing countries such as limitation of resources for the development of technical and vocational education, inadequate articulation between the training output and employment (qualitatively and quantitatively), illiteracy and the low level of general education, the lack or inadequacy of educational and vocational guidance services and the relatively low social status of graduates of technical and vocational schools. It was also mentioned that manpower assessment efforts are not able to analyse fully the requirements of the unorganized sectors of the economy, especially in the rural areas, which account for a large segment of the national economies in most of the developing countries, particularly the self-employment sector.

A specific problem seemed to be the lack of qualified staff including guidance counsellors for technical and vocational education. Well-qualified technical teachers in developing countries often find higher paid jobs in industry or emigrate to other countries with better financial prospects. It was also mentioned that in some countries the technical and vocational education teachers lack the industrial experience necessary for practical instruction. The lack or insufficiency of in-service training facilities for technical teachers was considered an important constraint in improving and updating the quality of instruction.

The problem of traditional and often irrelevant curricula was mentioned by several participants, especially from developing countries. It was stated that programmes are often copied from industrialized countries without appropriate adaptation to local conditions and needs. Reference was also made to the lack of harmonization between equipment and machinery in training centres and those of industries. The need for appropriate instruments for evaluation and examinations was also mentioned.

The attraction of suitable students to technical and vocational education was cited as a problem area. It was noted that in a number of countries technical and vocational education is considered a second or even a third choice. In this connection, it is important that proper attitudes and appreciation for this type of education and training are inculcated in young people as early as possible in the education process. The need for development of educational and vocational guidance was emphasized. Reference was made to the need for the improvement of selection procedures for technical and vocational education. Several participants mentioned the role of parents, especially in developing countries, in the selection of occupations for young people.

The special problems of girls and young women, drop-outs and the needs of special groups such as migrant workers and the physically and mentally handicapped were referred to by several participants. The limited access of girls and women to technical and vocational education as well as the problem of their lower status in employment and the difficulties in their mobility (especially in some developing countries) as well as the constraints of retraining were mentioned.

The special problems of education and training of migrant workers, taking into account their generally lower level of education, cultural differences and reintegration, were raised. In this regard, reference was made to the language problem and the need for specially prepared teachers and learning materials.

Several participants drew attention to the technical and vocational education and training of the handicapped and to their transition problems which are especially complex and difficult to resolve. The need for specially trained teaching personnel and learning materials to help the handicapped was stressed.

Attention was given to reforms in general education in relation to technical and vocational education. Both the vocationalization of general education (such as polytechnical secondary education) and the reinforcement of the general education component in vocational training programmes were discussed. It was felt that these are critical

Appendixes

problem areas which could, if properly dealt with, make a substantial contribution to the transition problem.

The problem of adjustment to changing requirements of technology was also discussed. In this connection, several participants expressed the opinion that a broad-based vocational education coupled with continuing training will facilitate the transition to these changes.

Current efforts and innovative approaches
The necessity for a comprehensive and continuing educational and vocational guidance system was underlined. Several participants described the various measures taken in their respective countries in this field. (The visit to two guidance centres in the host country also provided interesting experiences in this field.) It was recognized that aims, contents and methods of guidance and counselling require continuous adaptation to social and economic situations and their changes.

The importance of preparation of guidance counsellors and development of information systems about occupations and job opportunities (as well as placement services) was mentioned. It was stressed that guidance efforts should not be limited to the young persons in transition but should also involve parents, social groups and employers. Guidance services should take into account the particular problems of girls and young women as well as adults who have to change their work places.

The organization of different types of technical and vocational education and training was discussed. One participant felt that apprenticeship schemes are not often feasible in developing countries because the newly developed industries cannot cope with training requirements of young people. Another participant described a co-operative work experience programme which has been successfully applied in his country. The importance of research in developing new methods of training (such as the modular approach) was referred to by several participants.

The organization of polytechnical education and subsequent vocational training was also discussed. In this connection the participants had the opportunity to study the application of new methods and organization in relation to vocational education and the world of work through two study visits in the host country. One group visited an industrial enterprise (Henningsdorf) and the second visited an agricultural co-operative (Malchin).

The importance of co-ordination between education and training and production and employment at all levels of policy, planning and execution was underlined. Several participants described their national and local machineries for this purpose.

Possible measures for improving the transition
The symposium endorsed the suggestion in the discussion paper for national and international action and further suggested the following with a view to improving the problems of transition from technical and vocational schools to work.

At the national level
Arrangements for co-ordination of all national activities in technical and vocational education and training and improvement of management of technical and vocational education.

Efforts for a common policy among the government authorities, workers, youth organizations, employers and other social groups in dealing with the problems of transition from technical and vocational schools to work.

Organization of training programmes (such as seminars) for leaders of business and industry on transition problems.

Introduction of the concept of labour education, including information on labour laws, employment opportunities, etc. in the training programme.

Increased opportunities for retraining and further training; special efforts for the training of technical teachers and development of teaching/learning materials; improvement of working conditions and incentives for technical teachers.

Increased involvement of universities and teacher-training colleges in research and training in the field of technical and vocational education.

Attention to the harmonization and development of workshop equipment and machinery for technical and vocational education and training with those in industry.

Attention to the transition problems for special groups such as economically deprived, migrant workers, girls and women, physically and mentally handicapped, etc.

At the international level

Promotion of exchange of information on problems of transition from technical and vocational schools to work. Setting up by Unesco of a network of national institutions for co-operation on problems of transition; inclusion of transition problems as an item in relevant regional and international meetings concerned with technical and vocational education and training.

Encouragement of bilateral exchange of visits by experts from education, training, business and industry.

Promotion of norms and standards for curricula in technical and vocational education; organization of high-level international training courses specially dealing with management of technical and vocational education and training.

Promotion of regional and sub-regional co-operation on problems of transition, particularly in areas where trained personnel from one country find employment in another (e.g. the Arab region).

Increased inter-agency co-operation between Unesco and other competent United Nations Agencies on problems of transition.

Appendix 4. List of authors of country reports

Algeria, prepared by Amar Azouz, Secretary General of the Algerian Ministry of Labour and Vocational Training

Australia, presented by Ronald G. Ritchie, Acting Director of Technical Education for Victoria

Barbados, prepared by Ralph Boyce, Deputy Chief Education Officer of the Barbados Ministry of Education and Culture

Democratic People's Republic of Korea, presented by Ri Sang Soul, Director of the Democratic People's Republic of Korea State Education Commission

Ethiopia, presented by Mankelklot Haile Selassie, Head of Agriculture Department, Ethiopian Ministry of Education

France, presented by A. Bruyere, Inspector General of National Education of the French Ministry of Education

German Democratic Republic, presented by Dr Winfried Purgand, Director of International Relations of the State Secretariat for Vocational Education of the German Democratic Republic

Federal Republic of Germany, prepared by Professor Joachim Munch, University of Kaiserslautern

India, prepared by K. Sivaramakrishnan, Joint Adviser (Education), Planning Commission of the Government of India

Iraq, prepared by Dr Hashim Mohammad Said Abdul-Wahab, President of the Foundation of Technical Institutes of the Iraqi Ministry of Higher Education and Scientific Research

Nigeria, presented by C. I. Eli, Assistant Director of Education of the Nigerian Ministry of Education

Senegal, presented by Claude Journaud, Adviser to the Ministry of National Education and Director of Higher Teacher Training Institutes of Senegal

Sudan, prepared by Osman Mohamed Ahmed, Director-General of the Sudanese Department of Labour

Sweden, presented by Rolf Fak, Educational Adviser to the National Swedish Board of Education

Thailand, presented by Vivek Pangputhipong, Director-General of the Department of Vocational Education of the Thailand Ministry of Education

USSR, presented by Petr Novikov, Chief of Department, USSR State Committee on Technical and Vocational Education

United States, prepared by Daniel B. Dunham, Deputy United States Commissioner of Education

ED.82/XXXII.2/A